Junior Endeavor In Theory and Practice

by

Mrs. Francis E. Clark

First Fruits Press
Wilmore, Kentucky
c2015

Junior endeavor in theory and practice, by Mrs. Francis E. Clark.

First Fruits Press, ©2015
Previously published: Boston : United Society of Christian Endeavor, ©1903

ISBN: 9781621713357 (print), 9781621713364 (digital)

Digital version at http://place.asburyseminary.edu/christianendeavorbooks/

For all other uses, contact:

First Fruits Press
B.L. Fisher Library
Asbury Theological Seminary
204 N. Lexington Ave.
Wilmore, KY 40390
http://place.asburyseminary.edu/firstfruits

Clark, Harriet E. (Harriet Elizabeth), 1850-
    Junior endeavor in theory and practice / by Mrs. Francis E. Clark.
    232 pages ; 21 cm.
    Wilmore, Ky. : First Fruits Press, ©2015.
    Reprint. Previously published: Boston : United Society of Christian Endeavor, ©1903.
    ISBN: 9781621713357 (pbk.)
    1. International Society of Christian Endeavor. I. Title.
BV1426 .C6 2015

Cover design by Jonathan Ramsay

asburyseminary.edu
800.2ASBURY
204 North Lexington Avenue
Wilmore, Kentucky 40390

First Fruits
THE ACADEMIC OPEN PRESS OF ASBURY SEMINARY

Junior Endeavor
In
Theory and Practice

By
MRS. FRANCIS E. CLARK
Author of "A Daily Message for Christian Endeavorers."

United Society of Christian Endeavor
BOSTON AND CHICAGO

Preface

THIS book is designed to furnish a manual of methods tried and proved, for Junior Christian Endeavor superintendents and other workers. I claim for them no merit of originality or grace of diction, but simply the merit that they have stood the test of experience.

There are no theories set forth in these pages simply as theories. They have all been worked in many societies, and most of them have been tried in my own Junior society in the course of a good many years of work with and for the children.

One cannot wander around the world, and visit Christian workers in many lands, without consulting as to plans and methods, and whenever I have read or heard of a plan that promised well, or have seen it tried, it has been my custom, " when found, to make a note on," according to the suggestion of the famous Captain Cuttle.

This book has been made up in no small part from Junior methods thus collected from many wise workers, who have been able to lead many children into the Kingdom.

It is in the hope that these plans may in some way prove useful to others, that this manual of methods is sent out. I trust that it will be found worthy, not only of casual reading, but of actual study by young superintendents who wish to fit themselves for that difficult, but most blessed and rewarding, work of training the boys and girls for Christ and the church. It will, I trust, be used as a text-book in a correspondence school and in other ways by those who wish to make a special study of Junior methods as they have been found useful in actual experience.

Admirable helps for Junior Endeavor work have been furnished by Prof. Amos R. Wells, Mrs. Alice May Scudder, Mrs. Ella N. Wood, Miss Kate H. Haus, and many writers for many years in *The Christian Endeavor World*, but it has been thought by many that there was still room for a comprehensive manual of Junior methods, which should cover the whole field of Junior work, at the same time leaving out methods of doubtful utility and those that can be used only in exceptional circumstances.

The Junior Christian Endeavor societies are rapidly multiplying all over the world; the Master is blessing the faithful efforts of earnest workers for the children along these lines; and this phase of Christian effort gives promise of great and growing usefulness in the future. May this book add something, though ever so little, to the efficiency of Junior work and Junior workers in this wide field of Christian activity.

Contents

Junior Christian Endeavor.

CHAPTER I.

THE NEED FROM WHICH IT SPRUNG.

The Need So Strongly Felt.—Before beginning the story of the formation of the first Junior Christian Endeavor society and the resulting world-wide organization, and before we discuss its principles and methods, it is well to glance briefly at the work done for children in the modern church, and to consider the need so keenly felt a quarter of a century ago, which led to the formation of Christian Endeavor societies and later of Junior Endeavor societies.

It has been said that the religion of Jesus Christ is the only religion that has a place for the children. The first disciples, however, seem to have had little thought for them until our Saviour himself taught them the lesson that " of such is the kingdom of heaven." After his resurrection one of his last commands to Peter was, " Feed my lambs." Ever since that time the church has borne in mind the Master's command, and has tried, though sometimes feebly and ineffectually, and often spasmodically, to obey that command. It would be interesting to know just what efforts Peter made to

7

obey the command, but there is very little hint of his work in this direction in any of his writing, except an occasional message of tender love.

The Rise of the Sunday-School.—In the modern church there seemed to be very little thought for the children until at last Robert Raikes arose, and showed to the world something that might be done for them; and the church finally followed his example, until now there are few Protestant churches that do not have a Sunday-school where every Sunday children are taught in the Word; and many children and older people date the beginning of their Christian lives back to the time when, in the Sunday-school, a faithful teacher first opened to them the Scriptures, and led them into the love of Christ.

The Church and the Children.—But the Sunday-school reaches the children for only one hour in the week, and its province is largely to teach; there seemed to be a need for something more. After a time it began to dawn upon the church that the children might not only be taught in the Scriptures, but they might also be trained for Christian service; and, as the years went by, various organizations were formed in the church with this object in view, until there were in many churches Mission Circles, Bands of Hope, Loyal Legions, and various other children's organizations, all of which had for their purpose to enlist the children in some one branch of religious or philanthropic work. Many who are to-day among the most earnest Christian workers in the church received their first training in Christian service in some mission circle or other children's organization. And so, as the nineteenth century went on into its last quarter, the church became more wide awake to its duty to the children, and was trying everywhere, in many different ways, to care for the lambs of the flock.

Williston Church.—In the Williston Church, where the first Christian Endeavor society was formed, there had been from the very beginning of the church much time and thought given to work for the children and young people. Indeed, the church itself began in a Sabbath-school ; and a few faithful Sabbath-school teachers, with some of the young people who in that Sabbath-school had become Christians, were the first members from whom that church was formed.

The Mizpah Circle.—When the first Christian Endeavor society was formed, there was in that church a large and flourishing mission circle called the Mizpah Circle, which had been in existence for five years, and which had been trying to train its members for Christ and the church. At this time there were in the Mizpah Circle some seventy or more members, comprising boys and girls from seven to seventeen. Their special object was to interest all the members in missions, and also in their own church, in which respect it differed somewhat from most mission circles at that time, since it did other than missionary work.

It was the custom of the members to give every year a definite sum to their own missionary board, to be used as the board pleased ; but it was also their custom to do something, whenever they could, for their own church, and one large window in that church was the gift of that Mizpah Circle, whose members still look at it with pleasure, as they remember the days when as boys and girls they toiled to earn the money, that they might help to beautify the church. They also bought and presented to the church copies of the Psalms to be placed in every pew and used for responsive readings, and in many little ways, as they were able, they tried to help their own church, as well as their own missionary board. In these and other ways the children of that mission circle were being trained for Christ and the church.

But this mission circle did not seem to be doing all that ought to be done if Christ's command, " Feed my lambs," was to be obeyed.

Pastor's Class.—The pastor was sometimes present at the meeting of the Mizpah Circle, and he was well informed about every member of it. After the meetings of the Week of Prayer there were always some boys and girls among those who gave themselves to Christ, and the pastor felt that these boys and girls especially needed shepherding; so he gathered some of them into a " church-preparation class," that those who wanted to become Christ's professed followers might be ready, when their own hearts should dictate the step, and their parents should be willing, to enter intelligently and understandingly and sincerely into covenant with God and his people.

Each year after the meetings of the Week of Prayer this pastor's class was formed, and was continued for three or four months; and usually by the first of May some of its members were ready by their own wish and with their parents' consent and approval to unite with the church. I think it was in that

pastor's church-preparation class that the form of the
pledge which is now used for the Junior society was
first used. Each member of that church-preparation
class was invited to sign this pledge, and many of
them did so. As used then, the pledge was, I think,
as follows :

> " Trusting in the Lord Jesus Christ for
> strength, I promise Him that I will try to do
> whatever He would like to have me do ; that
> I will pray to Him and read the Bible every
> day, and that, just so far as I know how,
> throughout my whole life I will try to lead a
> Christian life."
> Signed_____

When afterwards this pledge was adapted to the
Christian Endeavor society, there was one sentence
added to it, which was substantially as follows :

" I will be present at every meeting of the society
unless prevented by some absolute necessity, and will
take some part in every meeting." The whole Christian Endeavor pledge as used to-day is really included
in this shorter one that was first prepared for that little
class of boys and girls, and whatever has been added
since has been only for the purpose of intensifying
and explaining the meaning of the original pledge as
the needs of the times have seemed to demand.

Other Methods of Work for Children.—But the
work that was done for the children in that church
was only a sample of the work that was being done in

many churches all over the land. Everywhere the church seemed to be waking up to the needs of the boys and girls. In some churches it had begun to be the custom to have five-minute sermons for the children every Sunday morning, and in others children's meetings were held ; and everywhere the question was, What shall we do more for the children ? The following words, quoted from Rev. Charles Roads, since Junior Christian Endeavor was begun, will show something of the feeling that had grown up in many churches.

" Who does not praise God for the teachings of Christ concerning children ? But let us beware, lest we fail to get his full loving purpose concerning them. The Christian world is yet far from looking upon children with the eyes of Christ.

" Writing for those who are learning, though late, to see somewhat with the eyes of Christ, we feel the need of a children's meeting supplementary to the Sabbath-school. We have nothing but praise for the enthusiastic and effective labors of the faithful teachers, now the rule in our Sabbath-schools ; and the love for Bible-study they have patiently developed is largely the cause of the present extraordinary interest in all biblical discussions.

" But the Sunday-school is ever a school, with a school atmosphere necessarily and properly in view of the importance of Bible knowledge, and cannot, therefore, satisfy the religious needs of the child any more fully than those of the adult. The Christian father and mother want a prayer-meeting, a testimony-meeting, and preaching ; and the peculiar spiritual help which these supply, in addition to the best possible Sunday-school, is also needed by the child.

" And as an easy transition to church-fellowship the children's meeting has an important place. . . . With due sense of the necessity of more direct and systematic work for the conversion and training of children, some time will always be found for the little company to gather.

" The church is coming profoundly to believe in the reality and power of a child's conversion, and in the clearness and joy of his salvation. The children's meeting is to deal specially with this young religious life, and to bring the child into actual church-fellowship by easy stages.

" Under ten years of age lifelong impressions are unquestionably made. Every adult has personal experience of some such impression. Shall we not, then, surround the child with the sunniest and most powerful spiritual influence? Moral and mental habits are begun and in building. Up with our scaffolding, and see that the soul is erected after heavenly drawings and plans."

Questions for Review.

(*a*)   What was the church doing for the children before the Christian Endeavor societies were organized?
(*b*)   What was the Mizpah Circle?
(*c*)   What organizations for children were in the church?
(*d*)   Describe the pastor's church-preparation class in Williston Church.

CHAPTER II.

Juniors in the First Christian Endeavor Society.—
When the first Christian Endeavor society was formed,
it had a place in its ranks for the boys and girls.
Nearly half of those who were its first members
came from the ranks of the Mizpah Circle, and were
between the ages of twelve and fifteen. They took
part in the meetings with the others, and were given
some work to do for Christ. Of course, the whole
society was an experiment, and it was not thought
wise to try two experiments at once; so there was no
separate organization for the boys and girls, but the
first Christian Endeavor society was almost as much a
Junior as a Young People's society.

The Christian Endeavor society was formed for the
sake of training up the young people in these two
cardinal principles: confession of Christ, and service
for Christ. The Mizpah Circle had done a good work
for the boys and girls, and they were all happy in their
work; but it was felt that the new organization might
wisely open its doors to them, and lead them into
larger and higher service; that, while they were being
trained to work for missions and for their own church,
yet this new society might teach them all that, and
also much more of Christian living and Christian service. In the new organization they would get a broader

14

training for all branches of Christian work, and it was felt that these things ought we to do, and not to leave the others undone ; so the Christian Endeavor society opened wide its doors, and the boys and girls of the Mizpah Circle walked in, and soon led in other boys and girls.

Origin and Growth of Junior Societies.—In other churches where societies were formed the same thing happened, till in many churches all over the land boys and girls and young men and women were being trained together for Christ and his church. But as the years went by, as the societies increased and their membership increased, and as their plans and methods of work became more fully developed, it was seen that there was not the opportunity to do for the children all that ought to be done. Many churches had held children's meetings of various kinds, and it was found that not only the older boys and girls, but even the little ones, were glad to come to these meetings ; and at last some one ventured to form a Christian Endeavor society simply for boys and girls, a society which should take in the little ones, and also keep the older boys and girls till they should be old enough to take hold more effectively of the work of the Young People's society.

Early Junior Societies.—It has been generally believed that the first distinctively Junior society called by that name was organized by Rev. J. W. Cowan of Tabor, Iowa, though others say that Rev. Mr. Savage of Berkeley, California, and others, that Mrs. Slocum of Iowa, formed the first so-called Junior society of Christian Endeavor. It is not easy at this late day to be sure which one was first in the field; but, be that as it may, it is certain that at about the year 1884 there were many looking about for some better and more definitely practical way of training the children for the service of Christ, and at about the same time several distinct Junior societies were organized, not far apart in time, though somewhat widely separated geographically.

Object of a Junior Society.—The object of the Junior society was the same as that of the first Christian Endeavor society, of which it was an outgrowth; it was " to promote an earnest Christian life among its members, and to prepare them for the active service of Christ "; and they all adopted substantially the same form of pledge as that used by the pastor's class of Williston Church in Portland, the same pledge that is used in Junior societies to-day.

Its Development and Success.—Of course the first Junior society, like the first Christian Endeavor society, was an experiment; but the part already taken by the boys and girls in the Young People's societies made the success of the Juniors scarcely problematical. The societies in Tabor, Iowa, and Berkeley, California, and the other early societies, proved to be not only popular with the children, but very helpful as a means of reaching the boys and girls and leading them while young into the love and service of Christ.

As the months went by, it was seen also that those who as children were so trained in Christian living and Christian service might properly be expected to become the best and most efficient workers in the older society when they should be ready for it; and, as the years have gone by, that has proved to be the case in thousands of societies all the world around.

The First Junior Rally.—These first societies were soon copied by their neighbors, and soon there were many Junior societies in America. At the Christian Endeavor Convention in Montreal, in the year 1893, there were so many Junior societies in existence that it was thought that there ought to be a children's hour in the great convention. Accordingly a time was set apart, and a children's service was held in one of the largest churches in that city. This service was found so helpful to the children and so interesting to their elders that it has been continued ever since, and now at every national convention, I think in every country, there is always a Junior rally. These Junior rallies at the State and national conventions have helped to call the attention also of those churches which had no such society, to the work for the children, and now these Junior societies have also multiplied and spread into all parts of the world till there are to-day more than sixteen thousand Junior societies in all the world.

What It Has Done for Children.—Before we go on to talk of the work of the Society more in detail it may be well to speak of some things it has done for the boys and girls of the world since the first Junior society was started, and perhaps from these results we shall be able to see more plainly the value of a separate organization for the boys and girls.

If the church committees all over our land could be consulted as to the children who have come into the church-membership in the last two decades, and how they have been brought into the church, I believe that we should find that the answer to the question, " When do you think you became a Christian?" will often be, as I have heard it given myself in many cases, " I think it was when I first signed the Junior pledge," " I think it was in one of our Junior Endeavor meetings," " I think it was in one of our little Junior after-meetings that I gave myself to Christ." Perhaps no one can tell all of the influences that have brought any one person into church-membership and into the active Christian life, but without doubt it can be shown that one strong influence that has helped many children into the Kingdom has been the Junior Endeavor Society. If it had done nothing else in these years than this, it would have fully justified its existence.

But, more than this, it has trained children in the expression of their Christian life.

It has trained them in Christian service. Many boys and girls have learned that *loving* Christ means *living* for Christ, being willing to give time and thought to his service. It has so trained them that many of them have in these twenty years become very efficient workers in the older society.

It has proved that it is as well worth while to train the children in Christian living and in the Christian graces as in music and the celebrated " three R's," and in gymnastics.

It has proved itself in many ways a valuable industrial training-school for the church; training the children not only in missions or temperance, but in missions and in temperance and also in Christian living and Christian service in many directions.

Look to-day into the membership of any church

which has for several years had a Junior Endeavor society, and you will be likely to find among its most earnest young members those who through the Junior society have been brought into the Kingdom and trained for service there.

Questions for Review.

(*a*) What place was there for children in the first Christian Endeavor society?

(*b*) What was the origin and object of the first Junior society?

(*c*) Where were some of the early Junior societies?

(*d*) Tell of the development of the society and its growth in America.

(*e*) When did the Juniors first have a part in a national convention?

(*f*) What are some things the society has done for the children?

CHAPTER III.

The Children's Age.—This has sometimes been called the Children's Age. It is the age of child-culture and child-study, of kindergartens and day nurseries and cradle rolls, and of children's clubs; and it sometimes seems as though a very large part of the thought of the world is given to the proper development and training of the child's nature, until the very children themselves come to feel that they are of great importance and value in the world. All these things are good, and it is well that the world is awake to the needs of the children; yet, with all the care and thought that are given to the children, there are in their education and training neglected corners that ought to be cultivated.

The Children's Education.—Our children go to school for five hours a day for five days in the week to study geography and grammar and arithmetic and other books, and then they go for an hour on Sunday to the Sabbath-school, and we think we are training them well.

In too many Christian homes children are taught to feel that the one most important thing for them while they are children is their education, and the inference is that education means only the education that they can get in the day-school. But what about their education in the Bible, and in Christian service, and in the duties of the Christian life? How much time do the children give to these things? Too often they are taught to feel that these are of secondary importance; that they *must* go to school every day, rain or shine; that no slight thing is to keep them away; that there is no excuse for failure in their lessons; their lessons *must* be learned; that is for them the important thing. But how is it when Sunday morning comes? Are they taught that they must be in God's house at the morning service; that no small reason should keep them away; that their Sunday-school lesson must be at least as carefully prepared as their geography lesson; that their presence in the church prayer-meeting should be the regular and expected thing, if they are old enough to go out in the evening, just as much as their presence at their day-school? Too often these things are allowed to take care of themselves, and a much smaller excuse is allowed to keep a child at home from the church service or the prayer-meeting or the Sunday-school than would keep him at home from the day-school.

Manual Training.—We think it worth while, too, that our children should learn to work with their hands, and manual training has come to have a very important place in the education of our children. There are sloyd classes in many of our large cities, and every boy in many grammar schools is allowed two years or more of this manual training if he wishes it. There are sewing-classes, too, for the girls; and in some places there are whittling-classes for both boys and girls, where they are taught to do very good work with their pocket-knives. Now all this manual training is very good, but why not also apply this same theory to their training in Christian living? Why not train them also in Christian work, and help them to realize that this is even a more important part of their education than anything else they can do? Why is it that in so many of our churches the number of those upon whom the pastor can rely to do the work of the church is only a very small proportion of the membership of the church? Is it not because they have not been trained in Christian service? They have never been taught to feel that Christian *living* means Christian *service*.

Training in Christian Service.—Are we not teaching and educating our children up to a very high standard of literary culture and forgetting to teach them to seek first the kingdom of God and his righteousness? The Junior Endeavor society is an attempt to look after these neglected corners in the education of the children, and to help them to put *first* things *first*. It is a kind of manual training-school of the church, where the children are taught to put into practice the truths that they have learned in the Sunday-school. They are taught the first principles of Christian living and Christian service. The whole work of the Junior society is to lead the children to Christ and train them to work for him.

Objections.—When Junior societies began to multiply in the land, objections to them quickly arose and multiplied also. It was said that children could not wisely take part in a prayer-meeting, that it would make little prigs of them, that they would be insincere, that they would learn to use words without meaning them, that the " glib " and forward children would have their faults increased, and that it could only be harmful to all children to be taught to speak and pray in meeting like their elders.

There were not wanting, too, those who said that their children were too busy with other things; that their education was for them the first and most important thing; that the object of that was to fit them for service; that, when their powers were developed and trained, and they were thoroughly educated, then they would be ready to take their place in the church life and work. Then there were endless objections to the covenant, and to the foolishness of asking children to promise what they never could perform; it was said that they would make promises only to break them, and it was wrong to ask it of them. All these and many more objections were brought up frequently and almost vociferously.

Answers to Objections.—The Society itself has answered these objections as the years have gone on. It has not raised up a generation of precocious prigs. It has not developed insincerity, if one may judge by the lives as well as by the words of the boys and girls who have graduated from these Junior societies in many churches; and I believe that, if the record could be made, it would be found that the children who have taken the active member's covenant would be found to have kept it much more faithfully than some church-members have kept the vows they made when they united with the church. The best answer to these objections is the Society itself and the work it has done for the children.   Choose a wise, winning, and tactful superintendent; give her all the help and counsel in her work you can; and then watch the results of her work with the children, and these objections will answer themselves.   But, though there is space here only for this simple answer to these objections, yet each one will be taken up more thoroughly in later chapters, where they will naturally arise again under other headings.

Objections from Other Organizations.—From the beginning the Society has had many difficulties to contend with.   Many have been found to object and criticise and few to help and counsel.   Even those who might have welcomed it because of sympathy in aims have held aloof and have feared that it would interfere with their own missionary or temperance work.   One difficulty that has arisen in many churches has been from the multitude of organizations that existed already.

It has been said, " We have now too many children's organizations; there is no room for another."   Yet those who have made these objections have not realized that this new society might obviate their difficulties instead of increasing them.   For, instead of adding a new organization to the number that was already too great, it has taken all these others under its roof; and instead of having a few children interested in missions, and a few others at work for temperance or in benevolent work, it has gathered them all into one society, and has set them all at work for missions and temperance and other good works, and has tried to lead them all up to the highest motive for doing all these things,—love to Christ and his church.

Junior Superintendents.—There has also been the difficulty of finding suitable persons to take charge of the society. This is not an easy work to do. It is not a position that would ever be coveted by those who would be at ease in Zion. It involves much labor and time and thought, and much of criticism where one might expect sympathy and help. The Junior superintendents do not receive salaries. It is hard work. Their one reward is in the consciousness of service done and the pleasure that always comes in working for the Master, and many of these superintendents will receive the reward promised to those who have done it " unto one of the least of these." Many churches are to-day without a Junior society because a superintendent cannot be found. The children are ready, but there is no one to lead them.

Training for Junior Work.—One great need of our churches to-day is the need of willing workers with skill and tenderness and tact, who have themselves had careful education and training in work for children. Why should there not be normal schools for training in this work just as well as for the training of teachers in the day-schools? There are some who are willing, but are not sufficiently well equipped for this service. Why should there not be in every church a training-school where those who would be glad to work for the children should themselves be trained especially for this service? This is to-day perhaps the greatest difficulty in the way of the Junior Endeavor societies that might be started in many churches. Trained, tactful, winsome Junior superintendents are needed; and, when they are found and trained, the children will be found ready.

But, though the Junior Endeavor Society has had to meet criticism and objections, though it has had many difficulties to contend with, yet it has made its way, and there has been a steady increase in the number of societies, as the years have shown what it is doing for the children.

Many churches and Young People's societies will testify that among their most valued Christian workers they count those who have had their training in the Junior society. I do not say that every child who has been a member of the Junior society has become such a valued worker, or that every society has accomplished all that was hoped and expected from it. It is as true now as it was in the days of the apostles that there are diversities of gifts, but it is also true that there is the same Spirit, and in a large measure it will be found true in many churches that the Junior Endeavor society is doing a valuable work for the children that the church was not doing in any other way, and a work that needed to be done.

Children as Church-Members.—In many churches children had been brought into church-membership, but there the church had stopped. Just when the children most needed her fostering care the church seemed to have failed in her trust, and very little in the way of guidance and training in the Christian life had been given to the children. Sometimes, indeed, it almost seemed that they had been left to feel that, when they were once in the church, it was all done, and there was no further upward step for them to take.

It was for such a time as this that the Junior Endeavor Society came to the kingdom; that the children might not only be brought into the church but that they might be trained for service there; that they might know that church-membership brought with it greater responsibilities and greater opportunities, and that the step into church-membership was only one step in the Christian life, which should lead the way into further and higher service.

Questions for Review.

(*a*) What is the present age sometimes called, and why?

(*b*) What is most important for children?

(*c*) What is the object of the Junior Endeavor Society?

(*d*) What difficulties has it had to contend with?

(*e*) What objections have been raised against it?

(*f*) Have any of the results sought for been accomplished?

CHAPTER IV.

Preparation for Church-Membership.—Most of our churches have come to believe that there is a place in their midst for the child. They believe in child-conversion ; and, when a child seeks admission to the church, the door is usually opened wide if there is good reason to believe that he has really given himself to Christ and is willing, so far as he understands it, to dedicate his life to Christ's service. But in many cases the church has done little or nothing to prepare the children for church-membership. The Junior society tries to help in doing this work for the church. The wise superintendent will not knowingly allow her Juniors to enter the church without having done what she can to help them to understand the step they are taking, and to prepare them for it, and will guard them and care for them so far as possible after they are in the church, that they may go forward into fuller and larger Christian living. Just how this work may be done in an individual society will be suggested in a later chapter. Here it can only be stated that in many societies it is known that this work is wisely and prayerfully carried on by consecrated leaders who are trying to do all they can for the children who have put themselves under their guidance.

The Children's Place in the Church.—The church needs the children in her membership. The church family cannot be what it should be without the children any more than a home that has no children can be all that a happy home might be. The church needs to feel its *responsibility* for the children, and it needs the help and inspiration that the work of training the children brings. It needs, too, the service that the children can give. For there are many bits of Christian work that the children can do, and the church that gives no opportunity for the service that children can render has failed of its highest mission.

The Church's Duty to the Children.—The children, too, need and should expect the help that the church can give. Christian parents should of course feel the greatest responsibility for their own children, and nothing can take the place of home training in the religious life as well as in every-day living and thinking. But what of the children who are not blessed with Christian parents; who learn nothing of the Christian life in their own homes; whose parents take the Sabbath morning for their Sunday paper and for extra sleep, and the afternoon perhaps for a Sunday excursion? What is to be done for these children, and what for those whose parents feel that their whole duty is done if they have dressed their children and sent them off to Sabbath-school; who feel that they can then shirk the responsibility for their children's instruction in the Bible, and trust it wholly to the Sunday-school teachers?

There is a large work that the church can and should do for the children; for those even who have Chris-

tian training at home, and much more for those who
seem to have no one to care for their souls. The
children have a right to expect that the church of
Christ shall care for them and lead them into right
paths. This the church is trying to do by her Sunday-schools, by her Children's Sunday, by her Junior
Endeavor societies and other work for children; taking them in, and guiding and teaching and training
them.

A Junior Society in Every Church.—But it may be
asked, Does every church need a Junior Endeavor society? Are there not other ways of training and
guiding the children just as effectively? To this it
may be answered that the one important thing is to
see that this work is done for the children. If the
church is already doing it in a better way, by all means
let it be known, and many other churches will be glad
to know of better methods. But, if the church is not
doing this work, if there is not a place in the church
where all the children of the church will feel themselves welcome, if the children are not being trained
in Christian living, if no one in the church is making
a systematic and consecrated attempt to gather in all
the children of the church, and to lead them into the
Kingdom, and to teach them how to work for Christ,
then that church which is not already doing this in a
better way ought to have a Junior Endeavor society.

If in any church there is really need of a Christian
Endeavor society for the young people, then in that
same church there should also be a place for a Junior
society. If the training that a Christian Endeavor
society gives is good for the young people, much more

is it needed for the children. Why wait till they are
young men and women before you begin to train
them for service? As well say: "We will wait till
they are fifteen or sixteen before we begin to teach
them arithmetic or geography. Instruction and book-
learning are good for young men and women, but we
will not give it to the children until they are able to
grasp it and understand it." If it is important to begin their school education when they are little children, much more is it important to educate them in
the things of the Kingdom while they are young.

The Juniors and the Y. P. S. C. E.—Moreover, the
older society needs the Junior society. The young
men and women are growing older every day, and
should naturally expect, as the years go by, to graduate
from the ranks of the Young People's society into the
life and the larger work of the church. Who shall
take their place in the Young People's society but
those who have been trained from childhood in the
Junior society, and may therefore be expected to be
ready to do good work in the older society?

It is said that one who wishes to reach a large degree of excellence on the piano should begin very
young, while the fingers are flexible, and should give
very careful practice as a little child if the best results
are to be attained. But which is of more importance,
to do good work on the piano or to do good work for
Christ in the world? Should not the same principle
hold true in this larger and more important work?
Does it not follow as a natural sequence that, if the
church needs a Christian Endeavor society for its
young people, it also needs a Junior society for the

children ?   It follows, then, like the parts of a syllogism :

Every church ought to lead the children into the Christian life and train them for service.

If the church is not doing this work in a better way, it ought to do it through the Junior Endeavor society until a better way is found.

Most churches are not doing this work in any other way; therefore in most churches there is need of a Junior Endeavor society.

Other Organizations.—But it may be said that many churches are already doing so much for the children through other organizations that there is no room for another. The children are already being trained to work for missions or for temperance through mission circles, Loyal Legions, and other organizations ; and all this is work for Christ, and will naturally lead them to loving Christ.   But, though this theory sounds true, and is true in a measure, yet, when put to the test of actual results, it proves to be true *only* in a measure. As a matter of fact, the children in these mission circles develop a certain zeal in collecting money for foreign missions, sometimes also for home missions, but perhaps not quite as often, and a certain interest in foreign missions ; but very little time and thought are spent in teaching them the common Christian virtues of obedience, truthfulness, unselfishness, and willingness to show their love to Christ by their lives at home.

And so with the temperance and other organizations. The attention of the children is turned largely to one phase of the Christian life, and they are not trained in the whole theory and practice of Christian living. They need to be brought to Christ first and foremost, and then taught that real love to Christ must certainly find expression in their lives at home and abroad, and in their work for others and for the church. This is what the Junior Endeavor society has for its declared purpose, and what no other of these organizations pretends to attempt. Look at their constitutions, and you will find their declared purpose to be to raise money for missions or temperance, and to interest as many as possible in that work.

All of these objects are good, and much has been accomplished by them, which has indirectly stimulated and helped the Christian lives of many children; but they are by their own declarations attempting only a part of the work that ought to be done for the children.

The following quotations from Miss Kate Haus, a well-known worker for children, who has been instrumental in leading many little ones into the fold, will show something of the distinguishing feature of the Junior Endeavor Society which differentiates it from all other organizations in the church, and makes it plain that it should supplement the work that other organizations in the church are doing. In some of our churches all of this work can much better be done by this *one* organization working for *all* the children, and by its means more children may be interested in missions, in temperance, and in benevolent and philanthropic work, and at the same time in the Christian life, than by having two or three separate organizations. In other churches, where the membership is large and the workers many, there may be room for these organizations to work side by side. Each church must decide for itself how it can best help the children in the midst of it, but in some way this broader and larger work ought to be done. But here is the opinion of this Christian worker who has led so many children into the fold: it ought to be carefully weighed by those who would do the best thing for the boys and girls under their care.

" To be able to hold the individual child after he has reached the age between childhood and youth is the place where so many of our Sabbath-schools fail to succeed. Children begin to feel their importance in the world about that time, and as there is nothing for them to do, as a rule, in the school, but attend, they drop out. The church sometimes gathered the youth and the child into its fold; but there it stopped, and felt itself powerless to do anything more, because it did not realize that there was a work for even the youngest member to do therein. Sent by God, the All-wise, the Christian Endeavor Society came to the rescue, and behold, the church found that it had a powerful force in its midst, and, setting it to work, great and wonderful have been the results.

" So, dear friends, this Junior Society of Christian Endeavor comes to you to-day, the last-born of God's blessings, intended to be used in gathering, saving, and educating the children for Christ and the church ; and I pray you do not put it aside, saying, ' We have enough blessings; this is superfluous.' There is no organization superfluous that will help save a human soul and fit it for God's work here and for his home above. Welcome it with open arms; bid it God-speed; do all that you can to help it on its way. Give it a place in your church home, your Sabbath-school, your heart of hearts, and, above all, a prominent place in your earnest prayers. It is that blessed baby that keeps all the other members of the family in sympathy with one another; and so it is the Junior Christian Endeavor Society that will keep the church in sympathy with the child, the youth, and all fresh young life. Welcome it as one of the watchguards that the Lord has placed in your midst to help you guide the footsteps of your little ones in the right path, and to make them strong to battle against the temptations that beset them on every side."

In a later chapter suggestions will be given as to how these organizations may supplement and help each other.

Questions for Review.

(*a*)   What is the children's place in the church, and who shall prepare them for it?

(*b*)   Why does the church need the children?

(*c*)   What may the children expect from the church?

(*d*)   Why does every church need a Junior society?

(*e*)   If a church already has other societies, does it need a Junior Endeavor society?

(*f*)   What distinguishes Junior Endeavor societies from all other organizations?

CHAPTER V.

The Leader.—In considering the formation of a Junior Endeavor society, the first questions that arise are: "Who shall have the care of this society? To whom shall we intrust this training of the children? Is there any one in our church who is fitted for this work, and, if there is such a one, is she not probably already too busy in Christian work to undertake anything else?"

This difficulty of finding a leader is the greatest one that has arisen in all the history of the Society, and it has seemed in many churches to be an insurmountable difficulty; and this is their only reason for having no society for the children. The boys and girls are ready, but there is no one to lead them.

But surely there is something wrong in the Christian church of to-day if it is true that the children are ready and waiting to come into the Kingdom, and there is no one to lead them in. Surely the Master says to us to-day, not simply, "Suffer the children to come unto me," but, "*Lead* the children unto me."

How to Find a Superintendent.—But how shall we find a superintendent, and who shall it be? It seems as though an angel were needed when we think of all the wisdom and tenderness and tact that are necessary for such a work as this. Some one has said, " Truly,

36

it would be an angel's work, but since we are not angels, and are not likely to find any in our churches, we must use the best material we have; and we shall find it is true again that ability is developed by service." Choose, then, for your Junior superintendent some one who has a great love for children and knows how to talk with them and help them, one, too, who is wise and winning and gifted. The work is worthy the best talent in the church, and the best person available should be secured; but, if for any reason the very best talent cannot be secured, then take the next best. "It is better that the work should be attempted, done in some way, than not to attempt it at all."

A worker in Australia who has studied this problem writes as follows:

The Ideal Superintendent.—"The ideal superintendent is one whose heart is suffused with Christ's love for little folk, and whose face is the playground for sunny smiles, who is both patient and persistent, with common sense enough not to lose her way in by-paths, and yet with ingenuity enough to keep out of ruts, who combines in her work speed with smoothness, who is both musical and methodical, and who has learned the meaning of that small and unaccommodating word ' *brief.*' Where is this worthy person to be found? Well, lacking the ideal superintendent, let us take it for granted we shall not find the ideal society. What, then, are we to do? Simply this: we must bring the real much nearer the ideal.

" Professor Jowett says: ' Difficulties may surround us; but, if they be not in ourselves, they may be overcome.'

" Alas! our greatest difficulties *are* in ourselves. A great deal more fitness is called for and is within their reach. My protest is not against mediocrity, but against people who do not see that they must make up for lack of genius by giving all diligence to justify their calling to high and responsible offices.

" The common sense of Christian Endeavor is that it enfranchises people with slender resources of gifts, but its covenant words—'strive,' 'try,' 'endeavor,' 'do '—lay vows upon us to overtake by consecrated industry the leeway of our adverse start in life. 'A man's real momentum is the product of his talents multiplied by his industry.'

" Suppose the natural gifts of a Junior superintendent may be represented by ten and her industry by two, she will not beat her neighbor whose genius is represented by two and her industry by ten. Dr. Arnold says, 'The difference between one boy and another is not so much in talent as in energy,' and those who have the oversight of our Junior work know that the difference between one superintendent and another lies not so much in talent as in energy."

Consider these words; and, while you look in your own church for the best talent for this work, look also for energy and industry.

It must be remembered, too, that sometimes this same example in addition may be worked out in a different way. For instance, if there is in your church some one whose concentrated energy and ability may be represented by two, there may be another one whose ability and energy are represented by eight; add these two together, and perhaps the result will be the ideal superintendent.

" You may perhaps find three people whose fitness for the work may be represented by three and two and five, and these three added together will bring the same answer." In other words, if there is no one in your church who can undertake the work alone, it may be that there are two or three or even four who can undertake the work together, and in the united efforts of these three or four there may be found more real fitness for the work than any one would possess.

More than One Superintendent.—Only see to it that they work together, not independently. Let them divide the work and the responsibility, but all should share in planning the work, so that it may fit together. I know of one society where three super-intendents work very harmoniously and helpfully to-gether, and their different gifts fit into one another so helpfully that the work is probably done much better than any one of them would do it alone. But it is their habit to hold frequent consultations together, planning the meetings perhaps for a month in advance, taking turns in conducting the meeting and feeling the whole responsibility for only one meeting in three, but planning to be present if possible at every meeting, and to help in any small ways as needed ; thus they keep in touch with the work that the others are do-ing, and, knowing each week just what was said and done in the last meeting, can make the next one sup-plement it wisely.

In some churches the minister finds himself able to take charge of this work, and, where he can do it, he finds himself helped in many ways in his own work for the church, for no minister can be in close touch with the Christian lives of the children without knowing better how to help their parents.

The Pastor and the Children.—In many churches, however, the minister feels that he is not fitted for this work, or that he has not time for it. In that case the superintendent must, so far as possible, keep him informed about the work and about the spiritual condition of the children, and call upon him occasionally for help in leading the children as opportunity offers.

The superintendent is sometimes chosen by the pastor and elders of the church, and sometimes it is left to the Young People's society to choose from their ranks some one who shall fill this office, and their choice is ratified by the church. In any case it should of course be with the sanction and approval of the church that the superintendent is appointed.

But it may be said that in some churches there seems to be no one qualified to do this work, and it is not even possible to find two or three who will share it. What then shall be done? It is indeed a deplorable thing if there is no one in the church who is willing even to attempt to lead the children into the Kingdom, but even so the case should not be considered hopeless.

If there is no one in the church fitted to be a Junior superintendent, manufacture one. In other words, fit some one for the position. It is possible to train up Christian workers for this position. The Correspondence-School, for which this book is meant to supply a text-book, it is believed is an efficient means of training Junior superintendents, and giving them the necessary technique of the work. Indeed, I see no reason why the time should not come when there should be in every church a training-school, where there should always be some one in training for the position of Junior superintendent and also for work in the Sunday-school and in the older Endeavor society. Appoint in the Young People's society a Junior committee, choosing those who by their winning ways seem suited to work for children, and then through their work in the older society, and perhaps by special counsel from the pastor or some older worker and by reading the literature on the subject, they may after a time be fitted to undertake this work.

Preparation for Junior Work.—A good preparation for undertaking this work would be to connect one's self with the nearest Junior superintendents' union. In some States in connection with the State conventions Junior workers' institutes are held, where real help and training are given. In most Junior superintendents' unions, too, there are very helpful discussions on questions of methods and work that will be very helpful to one who is contemplating this work. But perhaps the very best preparation that can be made is to prepare one's self. Given, energy, consecration, and a desire to help the children, and a superintendent can do much to fit herself for the position. Study the subject carefully. Read all the literature on the subject you can get. Attend some meetings of other Junior societies, especially those that you know are conducted by efficient, consecrated workers. Learn something from the mistakes that

other superintendents make, as well as from the wise
things they do. Consecrate your ingenuity. When
you see any new plan tried, or read of it, consider
whether exactly that plan or some variation of it will
most effectively help your own society. Attend the
Junior conference at your next State convention, and
you will learn much that will help.

Prayer as Preparation.—But, above all, be much
in prayer. Ask the Father himself to prepare you
for this work. Set yourself to do it *for Him*. Re-
solve to make it your first aim to help the children to
be Christians. Pray for grace to set them yourself an
example of the Christian life you would like to see
them living; and then, with your heart full of the
love of Christ and love of the children, begin the
work, trusting in Jesus for strength and wisdom to do
it wisely and earnestly and energetically.

Questions for Review.

(*a*)   Who should be at the head of the Junior society?
(*b*)   How shall the superintendent be chosen?
(*c*)   Should there be more than one superintendent?
(*d*)   What preparation should the superintendent make
for this work?
(*e*)   What qualifications should a superintendent have?
(*f*)   How can a Junior superintendent be found?

CHAPTER VI.

Organized Work for Children.—It may be thought by some that children are not capable of being organized for religious work, that they are too young and inexperienced, and that anything of this sort cannot rightfully be expected or allowed.

Yet, when one remembers all the organizations for other purposes to which children belong, why should it be thought a thing incredible that they can also be organized for *religious* work? There are children's clubs of various kinds, musical clubs and literary clubs and Boys' Republics, and it has been found that children through these organizations can do efficient work together. But these various clubs and societies are all of them for the benefit of the children themselves. Why, then, should they not also be taught to do organized work for Christ and his church, and thus learn something of the value and pleasure of unselfish work for others?

The Purpose of All Education.—And it is true that children need this training certainly as much as they need training in other branches of work. If it is worth while to give our children training in sloyd, and in cooking-schools and whittling-classes, and to have them spend hours in practising on the piano or violin or mandolin, that they may be fitted for the work they must do in the world, is it not also worth while to have them spend some time every week in doing work for Christ? But we need to ask ourselves once in a while, What are we in the world for? Who brought us into this world, and what does he want us to do here? Just what is it that the children are to be fitted for? What are their place and their work in the world? Surely all Christian parents must feel that their children have a work to do for Christ in the world; and, since that work is more important than any other work that they can do in the world, and since it needs more careful preparation and more skill and tact in the doing, it is plain that they should be taught and *trained* to do it.

Advantage of Working Together.—Most parents feel that they cannot wisely or properly train their children in music, in arithmetic, and in grammar themselves, but that their children will learn faster and do their work better if they are taught and trained in companies; and so schools have been formed, where thirty or forty or fifty children can be taught together. It has been found in many churches that the same principle holds true; that children learn more easily, quickly, and happily together; and that in some ways they teach one another.

The many Junior Endeavor societies that have already been formed have shown by their results not only that children need organization for religious work, but that they enjoy it, and that in this way they learn while they are boys and girls how to take their own little share of the work of the church, and so grow up into their own place in the life and work of their own church as a matter of course. One reason why it is sadly true in so many of our churches to-day that most of the work of the church is done by a very few people is, that the members of our churches have had this branch of their education neglected, and have grown up fitted and trained to take their own places in business and social life, but have never been taught to feel that they had any responsibility for Christian work.

They do not feel fitted to take up any benevolent or religious work, because, having never been trained to do it, they do not know how to begin. In future generations there need be no such excuse as this for not being an active and energetic member of the church.

Too Much or too Little Organization.—There have been many complaints in these latter days about our churches' being too highly organized, and about having too much religious machinery. Perhaps the fault is not altogether in the machinery, but certainly there should be a care in children's organizations that there should not be too much machinery. Just what is too much or too little organization can be determined by the individual church, but naturally the organization for the children should be a simple one, with just enough machinery to " make the wheels go round," and no more. A very simple constitution is all that is necessary, and only so many committees as will set all the members of the Junior society at work.

How to Organize.—A writer in the British *Christian Endeavour Times* has given so clear and concise directions for beginning a Junior Endeavor society that I will give them here :—

" Begin on the ploughed field of the Sunday-school. Let the children's ages range from eight to fourteen or fifteen years. Call the first meeting in a room which will be large enough to prevent overcrowding, and yet not too large for you to have adequate control of your audience. Be prepared for the first month to do a good bit of the talking yourself; but contrive some variety also, week by week—a straight talk from the pastor, a blackboard lesson from some efficient teacher, a Bible-reading and some reference-hunting ; these will be well within the general scope of your future work, and will attract attention.

" Take the names of all who attend the first meeting, and keep the register as you go. Read the minutes of the first meeting, however informal, at the next ; and in all things begin as far as possible as you mean to go on. Adopt a cheerful authority with the children; let them understand that you mean to be obeyed, albeit in all kindliness ; and insist on a reverent behavior in the precincts of God's house. Many a Junior society has suffered because this essential point has been overlooked in the beginning, and the difficulty of maintaining order remains one of the chief hindrances in the path of spiritual progress.

" Keep the pledge before the children ; explain it ; pray over it ; and then, when you believe the right time has come, after pleading with the children to give themselves to Christ, ask them to stand and show by repeating the pledge with you that they have yielded to the claims of his all-redeeming love. You want the children to take Christ before they can sign any pledge, and the way in which they respond to your pleading will help you to see how far they have grasped the fundamental principle of Christian Endeavor."

Do not be in a hurry to let the children sign the pledge, or to have too many sign it. Six active members who are earnest little Christians are better than any larger number who have simply followed suit, like sheep blindly leaping a hedge over which their leader has gone. All the rest of the regular attendants may still come to the meetings, and may, when you believe them ready for it, become preparatory members by signing that pledge, which will be given in a later chapter.

From the roll of active members let the children elect their own officers. With a little advice they will do it pretty wisely. Then let each do his own work, even though you may have more trouble in looking after them than if you did all the work yourself. It will pay best in the long run.

Necessary Officers and Committees.—The only officers that are necessary in the beginning are a president, vice-president, secretary, and treasurer. The committees can be appointed later by the superintendent, as she learns to know the children and is better able to judge which work is better for them.

Teach the children that it is an honorable thing to be elected to any office in the society, and that this honor brings its own responsibility. The Junior president should be taught to feel that his first duty is to be the very best president possible, to set such an example to the society as would naturally be expected of the president, to have the interests of the society at heart, and to help in planning how to make it a better society. He should be taught to preside at the business meetings of the society, and also of the executive committee, and should feel always that he is responsible for doing everything he can to improve the society. Let him feel that it is his society, and that he perhaps even more than the superintendent can improve it and make it accomplish what such a society ought to accomplish.

Officers.—The president may be either a boy or a girl; but, since such a position seems more naturally to belong to a man, and since every man in the church ought to be ready to do such work whenever it is needed of him, I would have a boy for president whenever it seems possible. It is true that oftentimes girls can be found who can preside at the business meetings better than any boy who happens at that time to belong to the society, and will quite possibly set a better example to the society; still, I would advise, whenever it can be done, to have a boy chosen for this office. Then, if he is not quite all that a president should be, help him to grow up into fitness for the position. It may be just what is needed to rouse him into Christian manliness, and it is quite possible that a boy who has been a leader in mischief can be trained to be a leader in Christian work, and such boys make the very best leaders when they have been so trained. Turn their power of leadership into right channels, and help them to see that this is a gift that God has given them to be used for his service, and so make them helpers in every good word and work.

The vice-president, too, should be a boy, if it can so be; and he might share the work of the president, perhaps taking turns with him in leading the business meetings, and helping in planning the work of the society.

Let the secretary and the treasurer be girls, unless there is some special reason why it should not be so; and teach them how to do efficient work.

Committees.—The committees should be appointed by the superintendent. At first have only as many committees as you need in order to set your active members at work; and, as the list of your active membership increases, the number of committees can be increased. It is quite possible to begin with only a lookout and a prayer-meeting committee, if you begin with only children enough for those two committees.

Let all the preparatory members consider themselves as belonging to the sunshine committee, and give them little pieces of work to do, that will help to put brightness into the lives of the aged or the sick or the little children or any who may be in trouble. The work of all the committees will be described more in detail in a later chapter.

Questions for Review.

(a)   Can children organize for religious work ?
(b)   What is the purpose of all education ?
(c)   What is the advantage of working together ?
(d)   What is too little organization ? Too much ?
(e)   What preparation should be made for organizing ?
(f)   What officers and committees are necessary at first ?
(g)   What children can be elected to office ?

CHAPTER VII.

Classes of Members.—A thoroughly organized Junior Endeavor society will have three classes of members, active, preparatory, and honorary. The active members should be those boys and girls who desire of their own choice to sign the active member's covenant, and should be allowed to sign it only after careful preparation by the superintendent, and with the consent of their parents.

The preparatory members are all those who with the consent of their parents will sign and keep the very simple pledge which has been prepared for them, and the honorary members should consist of any parents of Juniors who would like to show in this manner their sympathy with the work, and to help it as they have opportunity.

Active Members.—Of course the real strength of the society is in the active membership, and it should be the aim of the superintendent to bring into this membership as many of the boys and girls as possible, after first giving them very careful preparation; the superintendent should also do all in her power to help them keep the promises they have made. The covenant which is required of the active members is as follows :

> " Trusting in the Lord Jesus Christ for strength, I promise him that I will strive to do whatever he would like to have me do ; that I will pray and read the Bible every day, and that, just as far as I know how, I will endeavor to lead a Christian life.
>
> " I will be present at every meeting of the society when I can, and will take some part in every meeting."
>
> Signed

Of course no child should be allowed to sign such a solemn promise as this until there is reason to believe that he will try faithfully to keep it. Just how he may be helped to understand it, and to sign it sincerely, will be suggested later in this chapter.

Having once signed this promise, it should be required of all active members that they sincerely strive to keep it in the spirit and in the letter, and any child who appears wilfully to disregard it should not be allowed to remain in the active membership.

Preparatory Members.—The requirements for the preparatory members are much easier and simpler. They are expected only to sign the following pledge and to live up to its requirements :—

> "I will be present at every meeting of the society when I can, and will be quiet and reverent during the meeting."
>
> Signed

These requirements are such as any child can meet; and, while he is asked to promise very little, yet he is required to promise something, and to live up to what he promises. So much of purpose, at least, a child must have if he wishes to be considered a preparatory member of the Junior Endeavor society. The name " preparatory member " seems rather a hard one for a child, and a little cumbersome on account of its length ; but many earnest workers for the children have felt that it was a better word than " trial member " or " associate member," because it describes more exactly the relationship to the society.

A preparatory member is one who is *preparing* for active membership and for larger and higher service, and the very name itself helps to keep before the children the thought that this is not a permanent place for them, but is only a place where they can begin, and that as soon as they are ready for it they can be promoted to the higher and more honorable ranks of those who love our Lord and want to give their lives to his service. This thought should be kept constantly before the children, and the superintendent should be trying always to fit and train them for this larger place in the Lord's service. In a well-regulated society there will always be little companies of children, sometimes one alone, and sometimes two or three, or half a dozen or more, who are moving up into the active membership.

Honorary Members.—The honorary membership, as has been said, is for parents and older members of the church who desire to express in this way their sympathy with the work for the children and their willingness to help as opportunity may offer. They should become members at the invitation of the children, who should regularly vote them into the membership, as the active and preparatory members are voted in, at one of the regular business meetings of the society. It might be made one of the duties of the lookout committee to suggest names for this membership to the superintendent, and with her approval to present them to the society to be voted upon.

At least once a year there ought to be an "Honorary Members' Day" to which all the honorary members should be invited ; and there might be a carefully prepared programme for the children, which should be not very unlike their regular meetings, and should occupy half or a third of the time of the meeting ; and the rest of the time might be occupied by one or two of the honorary members who would be willing to speak a few words of counsel and sympathy to the children.

The Little Children.—But it may be said that a Christian Endeavor meeting where all the active members should take part, and where Christian work is to be done by the children, must of necessity be for older children, and there seems to be no place in this scheme for the little ones. Must they wait till they are eleven or twelve before they can have their share of the training ?

By no means. A true Junior Endeavor society will have a place in its life and work for even the very little ones. While the society cannot be made a kindergarten or a day nursery, or even a primary Sunday-school class, yet it should welcome to its meetings and its training any child, however small, who is old enough to come to the meetings, and sit quietly there and make no disturbance.

As a rule I think there is less danger of a disturbance of the meeting from the little ones than from some of the older ones, but a wise and winning superintendent will know how to hold them all in check, and help them always to feel that they must reverence God's house. Let the little children come to the meetings, then; and do not content yourself with simply allowing them to come, but invite them, and make them want to come. It is never too soon to begin to work for Christ; and the earlier you can begin this Christian Endeavor training, the better.

If it sometimes happens that one of these little ones is restless, and wilfully disturbs the meeting, say to him afterwards: " I am afraid you are not quite big enough to be a Junior Endeavorer yet, after all; but you are growing bigger every day, aren't you? Just as soon as you are big enough to sit quietly and listen reverently, you may come again, and I think you will be very soon. Why, you almost look as if you were big enough now! Do you suppose by next week you will be big enough to come and be just as quiet as the older ones? I have a great mind to let you try it once more, and see whether you are not big enough by that time."

Some such tone as this with the little ones will help them feel that it is an honor to belong to the society, and that they want to be counted in its ranks. It has been found that some who are very young are really in earnest, and can be trusted to sign the preparatory member's pledge, and so begin to be counted in as Christian Endeavorers without waiting till they are older. Try for the little ones, then, and train them up into Christian lives before they ever have a chance to wander away from the fold. In a later chapter will be found suggestions as to how the meetings can be made interesting and helpful to the little children as well as to the older ones.

What to do for Children Who Are not Members of the Society.—So far we have talked only of children who are willing to sign a covenant either simpler or more binding, but there are in every community some parents who object to pledges of any kind, and are not willing that their children should sign anything, even though the children themselves might not object. Shall such children be barred out? Surely that could never be the case in a society whose whole object is to win as many children as possible for Christ and train them to work for him. Every child who is willing to come to the meetings and to listen quietly, should be gladly welcomed. If some cannot sign either covenant, and so enter the membership of the society, yet they can come to all the meetings, and listen and learn ; and, if any of them are willing to begin by doing some work for Christ, something might be found for them to do as assistants to some committee, or as a special helping committee themselves, to do what they can to help any committee that needs them. Many children have really made their first step towards the Christian life when they have become regular attendants at some Junior Endeavor prayer-meeting, and from that have gone on till they themselves have become so anxious to become full members of the society, and to be counted among the Christian boys and girls, that the opposition of their parents has been overcome.

Let all children who wish to attend the meetings do so, simply making the condition that they shall be quiet and reverent, but do not call them members of the society until they shall have made the promises contained in either the preparatory or the active covenant. Help such children all you can. Make them feel themselves welcome at the meetings, and strive in every way to lead them to Christ, whether they ever come through the doors into membership in the society or not, but if possible lead them in time into active membership with the sympathy and approval of their parents.

In preparing the children for active membership the help of the parents and the Sunday-school teachers should, if possible, be enlisted. Call on the parents of a child before he signs the active member's covenant. Carry a copy of it to his mother yourself. Talk it over with her, and ask her to help the boy to keep it, especially by keeping watch with regard to the part of it that concerns regular daily prayer and Bible-reading and taking part in the meetings. Give her a list of the topics, and ask her to talk the subject over with her boy before he goes to the meetings, and to question him afterwards as to what was said there. The honorary membership will be a help in securing the interest and enlisting the sympathy and occasional attendance of the parents and teachers.

If you can enlist the active help of the mother, you have made a great gain for the child, and you have also helped the mother herself. Appeal to the Sunday-school teacher also, telling her what you hope for her pupil; and ask for sympathy and help in your work. If the two organizations are all that they ought to be, it should be expected that the Sunday-school teacher will greatly help the Junior work of the Junior superintendent, and that the latter will also help the Sunday-school teacher by trying to teach the children that real Christian Endeavor means endeavor in Sunday-school, as well as at home and everywhere else.

Questions for Review.

(*a*) What classes of members should there be?
(*b*) What is required of active members?
(*c*) What is required of preparatory members?
(*d*) Who may be honorary members?
(*e*) Is there any place in the society for *little* children?
(*f*) Is there any place in the society for those who are not ready to sign any pledge?
(*g*) How may parents and Sunday-school teachers be enlisted to help the children to be faithful?

CHAPTER VIII.

IT will be seen from the previous chapter that the covenant which the active members of the Junior Endeavor society are expected to sign is a serious one, involving earnest effort on the part of the child to keep it. The promises made in the covenant are these:

(1) I will try to do whatever Jesus would like to have me do.

(2) I will pray every day.

(3) I will read the Bible every day.

(4) I will try to lead a Christian life.

(5) I will be present at every meeting of the society when I can.

(6) I will take some part in every meeting.

The Covenant Promises.—It will be noticed that the first promise is a very general one, and that all the others are included under it. Any one who can sincerely promise that ought to be willing to make the other promises, which simply specify a few of the things that we believe Jesus would like to have us do. Yet there are many people, older as well as younger, who would readily make the first promise, and yet would greatly hesitate at the others, simply because the first one is so general. It is much easier for any one to say, " I will be good," than to say, " I will be

58

good in one definite, specific way." We are all willing enough to make the vague general promises. It is the definite ones that we shrink from. And if we stop and examine ourselves to see why we hesitate, if we are really honest, we shall too often find that it is because we do not really want to feel obliged to do these definite things regularly and unfailingly.

Bible-Reading.—I suppose that all Christians believe that they ought to read their Bibles every day, and in a general way they mean to do it, unless there is something to prevent or to make them forget it. But, alas ! too often there *is* something to prevent; and many Christians, if they would honestly consider the subject, would be surprised to find how many days go by without their reading their Bibles at all, and how many other days there are when they find time only to read hastily a very few verses. To those who honestly mean to fulfil this duty every day the Christian Endeavor covenant will prove what it was meant to be, a staff to lean upon, rather than a chain to bind. The very fact of having promised will serve as a reminder, until the duty becomes a habit, and the habit a real pleasure that would not willingly be given up.

But it may be worth our while to consider separately these five promises, which are all included in the first one, that we may see their reasonableness, and indeed their necessity for those who mean to live lives of Christian service ; bearing in mind that, if these things are duties for older people, they are duties for children too, and that their training should begin while they are children.

The First Promise.—If we have really given ourselves to Christ and have begun to live a Christian life, then we have already made the first promise, for being a Christian involves trying all our lives to do whatever Jesus would like to have us do. If there is any real love to Christ in our hearts, it is bound to find expression in our lives, and the more we love him, the more earnestly we shall " strive to do whatever he would like to have us do."

The Second Promise.—But most Christians would be willing to promise this and to let their children promise it. It is the second and following promises that cause more hesitation. But, if we really mean to do God's will, we know without any promise that we must ask him for help; we cannot do it in our own strength, and we need to ask him every day. As we grow more earnest, and stronger in the Christian life, we shall be more likely to follow Daniel's example, and at least three times a day kneel to God in prayer, rather than to have our prayers less frequent. Can we expect our children to form the habit of regular daily prayer and Bible-reading when they are older, if we do not train them to this duty while they are children? It should be a part of the care of every Christian mother to see that her children form these habits while they are young, and in this work the Junior superintendent can help her. This promise is meant to call the attention of mothers as well as their children to this duty, and to help them to do it.

The third promise we have already considered, and the fourth is also involved in the first, for one who has willingly made this first promise, and is sincerely trying to keep it, has surely begun to lead a Christian life.

The Last Two Promises.—The fifth and sixth promises are meant simply as helps in training children from the beginning of their Christian lives to be willing to make it known that they are Christians, and to learn, while they are children, in a simple and natural way to take their own part in the prayer-meeting by giving expression in words to their love for Christ, in a simple and natural way, as children may. It is too often the case in our church prayer-meetings of to-day that the whole meeting is carried on by two or three, or at least a very few of the older members of the church, the same ones every week, and the rest of the attendants at the prayer-meeting simply sit quietly and absorbed, getting as much good to their own souls as they may, but contributing little or nothing to the meeting to help others. If they had all been trained from childhood to feel that it was their privilege and duty to do what they could to make the prayer-meetings helpful to others, to have a thought of their own upon the topic, and to know how to express it, would not our prayer-meetings be greatly improved? These last two promises in our pledge are meant as a help in training up children in just this way.

How to Help the Children Keep Their Promises.—Though these promises seem reasonable and helpful, yet no child should lightly be allowed to make them. Different superintendents have adopted different methods in trying to make sure that the children are properly prepared to sign this covenant.

Three Doors.—The following method is one that has been tried with good success in some societies.

The way into the society is through three doors or gateways.

The first door is *Attendance at the Meetings.* Any child who cares to do so is invited to be present as often as he will at the meetings, and there is no condition made but quietness and reverence, that the meeting may not be disturbed. The children are encouraged to bring their little friends with them, even for a single meeting. The superintendent takes notice of these little guests, and makes them feel that she is glad to see them and hopes that they will come again. Many children have come in through this first gateway into the society, sometimes just for once, then more frequently, until at last they have expressed a desire to " belong," for all children like to belong to something. This first gateway is so wide and easy that it catches many children.

The Second Door.—The second gateway into the society is made a little narrower, but it lets the children inside the ranks of the society. This is the doorway into *Preparatory Membership.* If a child really wants to be a member of the society, he must promise something. It is not just a place for pleasure. From the beginning the children are taught that the whole object of this society is to make them Christian boys and girls, and to teach them how to show their love for Christ by working for him.

If they wish to be members of this society, they must begin to show at their very entrance through its door that they have a definite purpose in coming in. And so this second doorway is narrowed by two promises, but only by two, and those such that any child can make them. They will come regularly to the meetings, not simply now and then, not just when they happen to feel like it, but *regularly*.

If they wish only to come now and then, they must be contented to come only through that first doorway, as guests; but, if they want to " belong," they must come regularly, and must let no slight reason keep them away. That " when I can " in the covenant means exactly what it says. If they *can* come, they *must* come, if they wish to be members. If they are prevented by illness, or absence from town, or because for any reason their parents wish to have them stay away, then of course they cannot come, and they have sufficient excuse for absence. Of course no superintendent can go back of the parents, or in opposition to their wishes; but, when the mother thinks it best for a child to stay away from a meeting, whatever her reason may be, it is for her to decide the child's duty. This promise in the covenant is meant to keep the child's own conscience alive to his duty, and to make him feel that he ought to let no small reason keep him away from the prayer-meeting.

The second is also a simple and natural requirement. The children must promise to be quiet and reverent in the meeting. Even very young children may make these two promises, and so enter through this second doorway into the society.

The Third Doorway.—The third gateway into the society is much narrower and more difficult to enter, but the wise and winning superintendent will take the children by the hand and lead them through. This door leads into *Active Membership*, and into the Christian life. It requires from the children the promises given in the beginning of this chapter.

When the superintendent feels that there are a few among the preparatory members who are nearly ready for active membership, she gives a general invitation in the meeting to those preparatories who think they would like to become active members to stop for a little after-meeting to talk it over. Perhaps two or three children will stay, or perhaps fifteen or twenty. In this little after-meeting with only a few children she can get very near to their hearts. Then she explains to them very simply and clearly what it means to be a Christian, and how they may make the signing of this pledge the beginning of their Christian lives.

Often in this first little after-meeting some of the children take the first step into the Christian life. Then she tells them that for five or six weeks they will hold these little fifteen-minute after-meetings, and will talk over together the promises that they are going to make. In this first meeting they talk in a simple conversational manner about the first sentence of the pledge, " Trusting in the Lord Jesus Christ for strength, I promise him." She helps the children, by drawing out their own thoughts on the subject, to understand what trust is, and that it is only as we trust in Jesus for strength that we can make these promises, and that it is to him that we make them, and not to any one else.

At the other little after-meetings they talk over just one promise each time, and then the children are asked to take home a copy of the pledge and hang it up in their rooms, and practise this promise, but not sign it

yet. By the time four or five of these little meetings
have been held the children are generally pretty well
sifted out, and only those remain who are really in earnest. Those who stopped because others did, or for any
unworthy reason, are likely to get tired of these extra
meetings, and to give up after coming once or twice.

When the whole covenant has been talked over, and
prayed over in this way, then she gives the children
another week to think of it and talk it over with their
parents before they bring it back signed, and in the
meantime she tries to talk it over with the parents
herself, and to enlist their help in keeping the children
faithful. Then they bring back the pledge signed, and
are voted in by the society, after which all the active
members rise and repeat the pledge together; and the
superintendent or the pastor, or some one of the honorary members who may be there, offers an earnest
prayer that these new members and all of those who
have signed this pledge may be found faithful, and that
the Lord, whose they are and whom they have promised to serve, may keep them in his fold. Children
who have had this careful preparation for signing the
pledge are seldom found wilfully unfaithful in keeping it.

Unfaithfulness.—If, however, it is ever found, as
will sometimes happen, that a Junior is wilfully unfaithful, and does not seem to be even trying to
keep his promise, then it should be taken from
him. He should not be allowed to remain a member of the society, bound by promises that he is
wilfully breaking every day. In such a case, keep the
child for a little quiet talk alone, and ask him what he

thinks should be done. Appeal to his reason and his conscience; and, if this is wisely and winsomely done, he will agree with you that, for a little time at least, he ought to hand back his pledge, and have his name taken off the list.

But try to inspire him with a desire to begin at once to keep it again, that as soon as he has proved his sincerity he may come back into the ranks as a faithful active member; and then help him to do so. Let it be your aim to win him back again to faithfulness and earnestness in the Master's service as soon as possible.

Reorganization.—If a society has already been organized, and the children have perhaps been allowed to sign the pledge too hastily and thoughtlessly, then such a society should at once be reorganized on a better basis. Have a special meeting to talk it over with the children. Explain to them once more the purpose of the society. Tell them that it is not accomplishing that purpose, and you are afraid that some of them have signed the pledge too thoughtlessly, without quite realizing what solemn promises they were making. Give them a week in which to think it over carefully, and tell them that next week you will begin all over again, and they will all have an opportunity to take the pledge again if they really and sincerely wish to keep it.

At the next meeting pass around slips of paper to each child, on one of which is written, "I have thought about the pledge, and I want to remain a member of the society, and I will try to be faithful." On the other slip write, "I have thought about the pledge, and I think I had perhaps better wait a little longer before I sign it again."

Ask each child to sign his name to one or the other slip and to pass them in. After the papers have been collected ask those who still want to be active members to stop for a little after-meeting of fifteen minutes. Hold such after-meetings perhaps for two or three weeks, and at these little meetings talk and pray over the pledge with the children, letting them tell you just what their difficulties are, and what part of the pledge they find hardest to keep, and what efforts they are going to make to keep it now; and suggest to them means that they may use as reminders.

You will probably find your society much smaller after this reorganization; but, if it is rightly done, you will still keep all the others as preparatory members, and you will not be satisfied till the time comes when they are won back again into active membership that shall be a real thing and shall mean earnest effort to live the Christian life.

Questions for Review.

(*a*) What six things does a Junior promise when he signs the covenant pledge?

(*b*) Give a reason for each of these promises.

(*c*) Through what three doorways may a child enter a Junior Endeavor society?

(*d*) What can the superintendent do to help him keep his promises?

(*e*) What should be done if he wilfully breaks them?

(*f*) What may be done if a society has already been formed and the children are not keeping their promises?

(*g*) How would you reorganize?

CHAPTER IX.

THE JUNIOR COVENANT (*Continued*).

Objections.—From the very beginning there have been even more objections to the Junior pledge or covenant than to the older one. Those who have objected have been those who have not tried it, or who have not had opportunity to see what it has accomplished; but the objections have been sincere, and many of them natural ones. The Junior Society seemed in the beginning even more of an innovation than the Young People's Society. Children had been organized for mission and temperance work, but the idea of expecting children to carry on organized religious work and to take so strenuous a pledge was so new and startling that it is not to be wondered at that there were many objectors in the beginning; and, though their number has grown less, there are still many who do not understand how it can be wise to use such methods with children.

Most of these objections have answered themselves as the months and the years have gone by, but for the benefit of those who still meet these objections it may be well to consider them here.

A Solemn Pledge.—Perhaps the first objection that arises in the minds of those who are not familiar with the work is this: " It is so solemn a pledge, and requires so much of those who sign it, that it ought not to be asked of children. They will not understand its importance and its solemnity." It certainly is a solemn pledge, and should not be taken lightly, but a superintendent who has been wisely selected for her work will always be very careful to make sure that the children do understand it and realize its solemnity, before she allows them to sign it. This is the first principle laid down in all Junior Endeavor work, and reiterated at every Christian Endeavor convention and Junior conference and in every Junior Endeavor leaflet.

Do not let the children sign the active member's covenant until they have thoroughly studied it with their superintendent and have talked it over with their parents; do not let them sign it hastily or thoughtlessly; do not hurry them into signing it, or urge them; let it be their own choice. I cannot think that any one who has enough love for children, and enough earnestness and devotion to be willing to undertake this work, would allow the children to sign it thoughtlessly. As a matter of fact, I believe that the Junior superintendents are very careful and conscientious in the preparation that they give to the children for signing this pledge, using either such methods as have been described in the previous chapter or others that will accomplish the same object.

Faithfulness of the Children.—As one who has had opportunity to help to prepare many children for taking this covenant, I can testify that the children can and do understand its solemnity, and that they will freely and frankly talk over their difficulties and objections; and of the many children that have personally talked and prayed over the covenant with me before they signed it, in these last dozen years, as I have watched them and tried to help them to faithfulness in keeping it in the months and years that have followed their signing it, almost every one has proved faithful, and has seemed to be sincerely trying to do what he has promised.

I think their pastor would testify that, so far as any one can judge of another person's faithfulness, they are living up to their promises as faithfully as the older members of the church are living up to theirs. The children know it is a solemn pledge; but, though it is solemn, it is simple, and it is not difficult for a child to understand or to promise, and is nothing more than every Christian mother wishes her child to do, whether she is willing he should promise to do it or not.

Is the Covenant Pledge too Hard?—But there are now and always have been those who say: "This pledge is too hard. It is too much to ask of the children." Yet all Christian parents, and I believe even those who themselves are not Christians, wish their children to grow up as *Christians ;* and this pledge is only what Christ himself asks of his disciples. He says, "Ye are my disciples if ye do whatsoever I command you." That is all this pledge requires of the children—to do "whatever Jesus would like to have them do." It specifies a few definite things that he would like to have them do, and it is these definite things that most objectors find fault with, though none of them deny that these are things that Jesus would like to have us do. I suppose that every church covenant in the land contains a phrase that means very much the same thing.

A Church Covenant in a Child's Language.—I give below what might be called a translation of a church covenant into children's language, as written out by a girl of twelve who was a member of the Junior Endeavor society, as her understanding of the covenant she was to take in uniting with the church. This was the regular covenant that was used in that church, and after studying it with her Junior superintendent, and talking it over phrase by phrase, she had written it out in her own words as she understood it, that it might help her to understand just what she was covenanting in uniting with that church.

> "I humbly and cheerfully give myself to God in the everlasting promise of his grace, giving myself wholly to his service and glory; and I promise that by the help of his Spirit I will hold to him as my chief good; that I will be faithful to the public services of his church, and in Bible-reading and prayer; that I will seek the honor of his name; that I will try to lead others to him, and will work for his kingdom, giving up everything that will draw me away from Christ. . . . I do now cordially join myself to this church and promise to live by its rules; and I solemnly promise to do all I can for its interests."

All this is either plainly written or implied in almost every church covenant, and yet there are those who will allow children whom they believe to be Christians to take this covenant, even while they are objecting that this Junior Endeavor covenant is too hard.

Perhaps, however, the best answer to these objectors is the fact that it has not proved too hard for any child who sincerely wishes to lead a Christian life, and that many have taken their first step into the Christian life when they have conscientiously and intelligently signed this pledge and have faithfully tried to live up to its requirements.

Objections to Making Promises of Any Kind.—But there are always some who object to signing any pledge. They say that they will not sign pledges themselves, and will not allow their children to do so. Yet these same objectors have made very solemn and binding promises themselves when they took their marriage vows, and are every day signing business contracts and making promises that are just as binding as these in the pledge.

Too often the real objection to taking this pledge is that people do not want to feel obliged to keep these promises. They do not want to think they must do these things regularly and faithfully. Let us ask the objecting parent a few questions. If you wish your child to read his Bible and pray every day, and to attend his prayer-meeting faithfully, and take his share of the work, if you intend to have him do these things, why should you object to having him PROMISE to do them? Can it be that you do not intend to have him attend regularly to his Christian duties, that you are afraid to let him *promise* to do them? Would you be afraid to let him promise that he would go to school every day when he could, and would study his lessons there? You know that you intend to have him do that; and, if he were asked to promise it, you would not be at all afraid of the promise, for you mean to have him do it whether he promises or not. If you just as really and thoroughly meant that he should grow up a Christian and should take his share in the church life and work, would you be afraid to have him promise to do it? These questions are worth thinking over carefully and answering honestly.

Can a Child Keep These Promises?—But there are honest objectors who say, "It is not that I am afraid of promises, but these are such solemn ones that I am afraid he will not keep them." True, there is a danger; but, if these are things that he ought to do, it should be our duty to help him keep them, rather than to hinder him from making them at all.

As has been said before, the promise should be considered as a staff to lean on, not a chain to bind; and we ought to let the children have the staff. Teach them the solemnity of the promise, but also the joy of it; and then help them to keep it. Make it your own duty and privilege to see that they do not break it.

How to Help the Children Keep Their Promises. —The superintendent can do much to help the children keep their pledge by frequently talking it over with them and explaining it, and finding out their difficulties, and encouraging them, and giving them little reminders; but the parents who see them every day can do far more to help them keep it. Ask yourself this question, then, and answer it honestly in God's sight: Which will be better for my child, to prevent him from signing this pledge, because of the fear lest he may break it, or to show him that these are things that he ought to do whether he promises or not, and to encourage him to promise, because the very promise will be a help and a reminder

to him, and then to feel my own responsibility for
him, and to help him keep it? Which plan will
be more likely to make an earnest working Christian
of him? Is that what you want him to be?

Bible-Reading.—But I have often met those who
have no objections to the other promises of the
pledge, but who say: " I am afraid the children will
not remember to read their Bibles every day. They
never will keep this part of the pledge, and they must
not promise it."

I always wonder whether those who make this
objection do read their own Bibles every day, and
whether they are training their children to do it.
They want the children to lead a Christian life, but
how can they expect them to do it if these children
are not in the habit of studying God's word every day
for counsel and direction, and praying to him for help
to obey its teachings? How can they know what is
God's will for them if they do not look for it in his
word?

There are certain duties that we teach a child
to perform every day, that we should not think
of letting him neglect, even if he should forget
them himself. We expect him to wash his face and
brush his hair, for instance, every morning before he
appears at the breakfast-table. Is this more important than that he should look to God for guidance, and
read a few words from His book? If we can teach
him to wash his face every morning, can we not
also teach him to read his Bible every morning, if we
think it as important and take as much pains about it?

How often in the day do we ask him whether

he has washed his face or hands? How often do we
ask him whether he has read his Bible? How often
do we mothers go ourselves and wash the child's face
or hands for him? How often do we read the Bible
with him?

Let parents ask themselves some of these practical
questions, and then consider whether they have
any right to say that their boys will not keep this
promise.

But there are children who have not Christian
parents. Should such be allowed to sign this pledge?
Not until you are persuaded that they mean to do the
things they promise. It will be harder for such children, and the superintendent must strive to exert
a stronger influence, and give more frequent and
more careful help; but I have so often known children
of non-Christian parents to form this habit for themselves, and faithfully to keep this promise, that I
am sure there are many such who may be taught
to do this thing, and that even this part of the pledge
need not be alarming with proper care and guidance
on the part of superintendent and Sunday-school
teacher.

Taking Part in the Prayer-Meeting.—Still one
other objection often arises. For there are those who
say: " There is no need of their promising to take
part in the prayer-meeting. It will make them insincere. They will say what they do not mean, or they
will become priggish or conceited."

There is a danger here, though it is usually greatly
overestimated. But like the others it can be guarded
against. This, too, is a cardinal principle of Junior

Endeavor, which is learned, I believe, by every Junior superintendent at the beginning of her work, and is reiterated at every convention and conference. " Be very careful how your Juniors take part in the meeting. Teach them to say only what they really mean. Teach them not to pray unless they really have something for which they wish to ask, or blessings for which they really wish to thank their Father." Show them how to have a thought on the topic which they can express simply and naturally. Help them to see what is the most helpful and sincere way to take part in a prayer-meeting.

Just how they may be taught to do this in the most helpful way, or at least some methods by which they may be helped, will be given in a future chapter on the prayer-meeting. Perhaps it is sufficient to say here that as a matter of fact it has proved that children do take part simply and naturally, and that their childish prayers seem to be as earnest and sincere as any that can be heard in the church prayer-meeting.

It remains true, then, as a natural and logical fact that, if prayer-meetings are desirable for the church, some one must be ready to take part in them; and it naturally follows that those who have been trained from childhood to do this will be likely to do it more helpfully than those who must hesitatingly and timidly begin to do it as a wholly unaccustomed duty when they are older and their habits of thought and speech formed.

Only let it be remembered that especially in a children's meeting taking part does not mean an exhor-

tation or a learned discourse, but rather the expression
of a simple, helpful thought on the topic, or a very
short, simple prayer for definite help that is desired, or
a childlike expression of thanks for definite blessings
received.

With this thought in mind, experience has proved
in all these years that children can be taught to take
part in the prayer-meeting simply and naturally, without conceit or unpleasant precociousness, and that as
they grow older they are better able to take their place
in the church prayer-meeting because of the training
they have had as Juniors.

Questions for Review.

(*a*) What answer would you give to those who say,
"The children do not understand the solemnity
of the pledge "?

(*b*) What to one who says, " It is too hard for them " ?

(*c*) What to one who says, " They ought not to sign
any pledge " ?

(*d*) What to one who says, " They will not keep their
promises " ?

(*e*) What to one who says, " They might keep the
other promises, but they will not remember to
read their Bibles every day " ?

(*f*) What to one who says, " They will learn to be insincere " ?

(*g*) Will it make them priggish ?

CHAPTER X.

The Prayer-Meetings.—A true Junior Endeavor society should usually hold a prayer-meeting as often as once a week, unless in exceptional circumstances. These meetings should be real prayer-meetings, conducted as nearly as may be like the meetings of the Young People's society. It is for each church to decide for itself what day is the best for the Junior meetings, but there are many reasons why it would seem better that the meetings should be held if possible on a week-day and in the afternoon, or as early as possible in the evening.

When to Hold the Meetings.—Many societies hold their meetings on a week-day afternoon, immediately after school. In some churches it is the custom to have the meetings on Sunday afternoon, but there are so many objections to this time that the matter ought to be very seriously considered before this time is selected. The Sunday is always a crowded day, with Sabbath-school and preaching-service and evening service and young people's meeting. Often, too, it happens that the Junior superintendent is also a Sunday-school teacher and a member of the Young People's society, with many other duties to fill up her Sunday, and it ought not to be expected of her to fill up her last possible opportunity of rest on the Lord's Day with the Junior Endeavor meeting. Moreover, it is not a good thing for the children to feel that they can crowd all their religion into the Sunday, and that they cannot give up any of their playtime for religious work. For the sake of teaching them this lesson, if for no other reason, it seems desirable that their meetings should be held on a week-day.

On the other hand, it is sometimes said that in many of the cities and other places where the society has been formed in connection with city-mission work it helps to keep the children out of the streets on Sunday, and that their mothers are glad to have them taken care of on Sunday afternoons. But even in these cases the fact remains true that these children need to learn to give up some of their playtime to the Lord's service.

Would it not be better for them also to have a part of their religious instruction during the week, instead of putting it all into the Sunday? Let the Sunday-school teacher give them all the help and uplift she can on Sunday, and then on Wednesday or Thursday or Friday let the Junior superintendent try to help them to put in practice what they learned on Sunday.

Of course there should be no hard and fixed rule for all societies, and there may be many societies which can best hold their meetings on Sunday, but the whole subject ought to be carefully considered, and then settled in the way that will be most helpful for the *children;* for they are the ones to be helped and trained.

Whatever day is chosen, try to help the children to

feel that that is their day, and a time to be looked forward to with pleasure.

Length of Meetings.—The meetings, on whatever day they may be held, should not be too long. Ordinarily about three-quarters of an hour is as long as the children can profitably be held. A short helpful meeting is much better than one that continues till the children are weary and longing for the meeting to close. They can learn as much as they can hold in a shorter time, and will remember it better. A good prayer-meeting should always begin promptly and close promptly, and then the children will know just what to expect.

Moreover, if your meetings are short, it will leave opportunity for an occasional short after-meeting for just two or three whom the superintendent can reach more easily if she has them by themselves. If a society is large, the meetings must of necessity be somewhat general in their character, but very often a short after-meeting for those who would like to stay to talk about beginning the Christian life, or to prepare for active membership, may be made a very helpful adjunct to the prayer-meeting.

Taking Part in the Prayer-Meeting.—There have been many to object to the plan of having the children themselves take part in the prayer-meeting. But how shall they learn to do it when they are older if they are not trained to it? Will it not be easier for them by and by, and will they not know how to do it more helpfully, if they learn to do it while they are young, and if it becomes a matter of course to them to take their own share of the prayer-meeting? This

matter of taking part in the meeting need not be made
a great bugbear. To take part in a prayer-meeting is
to say something in the meeting, or to offer a prayer ;
but it is not necessary to say something very wise or
very eloquent, or to offer a long and " able prayer."

A child who has repeated a Bible verse, or expressed a single thought on the topic, or offered a
simple petition for blessing or help or forgiveness, has
taken part in the meeting. One object of this society
is to teach the children how to take part in the meeting sincerely and helpfully, and a great part of the
work of the superintendent is so to plan the meeting
that she can help the children to take their part.
Sometimes she will write four or five questions on the
topic on the blackboard, and let any who choose take
part by answering these questions.

How to Help the Children Take Part.—Sometimes
she will ask each one to bring a Bible verse on the
topic, and to tell in his own words what he thinks it
means, or how it has helped him. Sometimes she
will make the meeting conversational, and let the
children take part by answering questions she may
ask them as the meeting goes on. Sometimes she will
give them a Bible story, or a story of missionary life,
to learn and tell in the meeting. In all these and
many other ways she will teach them how to think
over the topic themselves, and have something to say
about it.

Praying in the Prayer-Meeting.—The question of
asking the children to pray in the meetings is a more
serious one. It is so easy for older people as well as
for children to let their prayers become mere words,

without an earnest desire for the blessings they ask, that one should try in every way to guard the children from insincerity. Always remind them that praying is talking to God. Always wait till the room is very quiet before you allow prayer to be offered. Teach the children to take a reverent attitude in prayer. Do not *urge* the children to pray, but rather let only those pray who have something definite to pray for. Sometimes give them Bible prayers to read and then to make their own if they can say them sincerely. Let them have a moment of silent prayer before the audible prayers begin, that they may ask God to make them sincere in their praying. Sometimes ask their prayers for special objects, but first interest them in these objects, so that they may really desire the blessings they ask.

Sincerity in Prayer.—Try above all things to guard them from insincerity in prayer. And I believe this may be done, and that as a rule the children's prayers are quite as earnest and reverent and sincere as those of their elders, so far as one who does not see the heart can judge; and this belief has come to me as a result of years of work with children, and because of their prayers that I have listened to and joined in.

The Superintendent's Part in the Meeting.—The superintendent's part in the meetings should always be bright and brief. Whether you think it best to let one of the children lead the meeting, or to lead it yourself, make your own part brief. Study to say what you have to say, in such a way that it must hold the children's attention; and, when you cannot hold it, stop talking.

Illustrate your point with a bright story or with some object, or with the blackboard when you can in this way make it plainer; but think of these methods only as tools, to be used when they will help, but never to be used for their own sake alone. Do not be tied to blackboard work, or object teaching, or even to story-telling. Have a point to make, and make it in the best and brightest and most earnest way you can. Sometimes use one of these methods and sometimes another; but make your point every time, and give the children something to remember that will help them. Sometimes lead the meeting yourself; sometimes let your part of it be only a ten minutes' talk on the topic; sometimes content yourself with a general oversight of the meeting, and ask some one else to talk to the children; but do not omit their part in it.

The Bible in the Meetings.—See that the children have their Bibles in the meeting quite frequently, if not always, and sometimes give out references for them to find, or passages for them to read, or have a responsive reading on the topic. But do not let them form the habit of taking their own part in the meeting simply by reading a Bible verse. If they wish to take part in the meeting in Bible words, let them learn their verses and repeat them.

The Object of All the Meetings.—But let it not be forgotten that the whole object of these meetings is worship. Sometimes even in the use of good methods there is danger that this may be forgotten. Help the children to feel that for a half or three-quarters of an hour they are going to worship God, and that he is there with them, that they will talk to him, and that he will listen as they talk of the topic together. Be very careful to have the meeting always reverent, and to make the children feel that this meeting is to them what the church prayer-meeting is to the older members of the church.

It follows, then, as a matter of course that there must be order in the meetings, or there cannot be worship. How to secure order is the problem that confronts every superintendent and leader of children's meetings; but in some way it must be secured, and the leader who cannot do it has mistaken her vocation, or she has allowed her children to become members without considering the pledge sufficiently, or she has not been firm enough. It needs consecrated ingenuity and tact, but it is possible to find something for the mischievous ones to do, and to make it so interesting that the indifferent ones must listen.

Special Meetings.—Sometimes much good can be done by holding special meetings that bring together only a few children, or certain selected ones. I have already spoken of after-meetings that may be held for those who wish to become active members. Sometimes hold these little after-meetings for those who want to know how to begin to be Christians, sometimes for those who want to unite with the church, but need special preparation; sometimes hold little evangelistic meetings.

Take special pains in preparing the consecration meetings, to make them solemn and helpful. But the one object of all these meetings should be that of the whole society,—to lead the children to Christ and train them for his service. Sometimes hold a meeting specially for boys, and let the pastor, or perhaps some bright, popular, earnest young man whom they all respect, come and help in the meeting.

Sometimes hold a meeting for the girls, and sometimes one for the older members or for the very youngest ones; but do not let these little meetings interfere with the regular meetings of the whole society together. These should be only occasional meetings, held before or after the regular meetings, which may be shortened a little to allow time for it; or sometimes one of these little special meetings might be called at a special time apart from the regular meeting. But, like all the other methods, these should be used wisely, and only when they are needed and will prove really helpful.

Often where a society is large, with a good many little children, it is wise to divide the society, having a sub-Junior meeting for those under ten or under nine, letting the opening services be for all, and then marching out the little ones to the tune of " Onward, Christian Soldiers," into another room, to hold a shorter meeting at the same time and on the same topic, so that they may still feel that they are a part of the society. In some churches it may be wiser to have two Junior societies.

Questions for Review.

(*a*) How often should the prayer-meetings be held, and on what day?

(*b*) How long should the meetings be, and how conducted?

(*c*) How can the children be taught to take part in the meetings?

(*d*)   How can the children be taught to pray in the
meetings?

(*e*)   What is the superintendent's part in the meeting?

(*f*)   How may the children use their Bibles in the
meetings?

(*g*)   How is the element of worship secured?

(*h*)   How would you secure order in the meetings?

(*i*)   What special meetings may be held?

CHAPTER XI.

Importance of Business Meetings.—A Junior Endeavor society should have its business meetings as regularly as the Young People's society, and they should be conducted in as businesslike a manner. The children should be taught to feel the importance of these meetings and to conduct them themselves. A Junior president ought to be so trained and taught that sometime he will make a very good president for the older society if he is needed for that position, and it is well that he should learn the duties of that office while he is a boy. The same efforts should also be made to train the other officers of the society.

When to Hold the Business Meeting.—The business meetings should be held at least as often as once in two months, and oftener if in any society it seems best. Some societies hold them once a month. Some societies make these separate meetings, or hold them in connection with sociables, and others hold them in connection with the prayer-meetings. Each society must decide for itself just when these meetings shall be held, and it should depend somewhat upon the nature of the business transacted.

How to Conduct It.—Usually a business meeting will mean only the hearing of the reports of the secretary and the different committees, and the voting in of any new members who may have been proposed. The children should be helped to write their reports, that they may make them a brief record of work attempted or planned for the future, or perhaps sometimes simply a confession of little work attempted, and the expression of a purpose to do better work in the next month. The reading of these reports may be made a most helpful part of the meeting, and it may be found wise to take the first fifteen minutes of the prayer-meeting for a devotional business meeting, when the children shall tell of the work they have attempted or have failed to do, and shall be reminded that all this work is for Christ and his church, and that by doing it efficiently and promptly they are pleasing him and learning to be more useful in his service; and it may well close with prayers that they may be "not slothful in business, fervent in spirit, serving the Lord." Such a business meeting as this might always be held in connection with the regular prayer-meeting if it were thought best. If, however, the business meeting is to consider new plans of work, or plans for raising money, or anything which you wish the Juniors to discuss themselves, then it might more properly be held for the first half-hour of a sociable, or at some special meeting called for the purpose.

The Question of Finances.—Naturally there will not be very much business to be transacted at the Junior business meetings, but there should be enough to train the children in businesslike ways of doing their work, even Christian work. The question of the society finances might wisely be discussed with the children at some business meeting early in the year's work, taking this up in connection with a sociable. Let the children express their own opinions on such questions as these: What money do we need in our society? What is the best way to raise our money? What proportion of the money we raise ought we to use for ourselves? How can we most wisely distribute the money that we give away? What proportion of it should we give to foreign missions, and what to home missions, and what to city missions? What proportion of our foreign or home missionary money should go to special objects which are sometimes presented to us, as fresh-air missions, comfort-bags, the poor of our own town, and what to the general work of the boards? If you can train the children to think for themselves on these topics, and to give their money systematically, and with a wise proportion, you will have done for them what ought to have been done for the older members of our churches, and will have helped to solve some of the problems of our missionary boards in the days when these boys and girls of ours shall be older.

Society Methods.—Sometimes, too, discuss with the children questions in regard to the best methods to be used in the society, and get their own ideas as to the best kind of prayer-meeting, the best kind of business meeting, the best ways of maintaining order and reverence in the meeting, the best ways of gaining and admitting new members, the best ways of keeping the society in good working order. If you have not tried it, you may be surprised to find what wise ideas of order and good government the children have. Such meetings as these, however, should be only occasional, and at the usual business meetings there should not be much business transacted except the reading of the reports and the reception of new members.

Reports of Committees.—Be very particular about these reports, that they shall always be written, and that they shall be honest. It will mean some labor on the part of the superintendent as well as of the children, but it will help them to feel their responsibility for their work, and the very fact that they must report to the society the manner in which they have done the work committed to them will in itself incite them to do better work.

The Chairman.—Let the Junior president preside at these business meetings, or let him take turns with the vice-president, that they may both know better how to do this work. Teach the little president how to preside in a dignified and businesslike way. Let him, if need be, rehearse a business meeting beforehand with the superintendent, or with his father and brothers, that he may speak promptly and distinctly, and call for reports and votes in a manly, businesslike way. Always have a report from the secretary at these business meetings, and occasionally from the treasurer. Always open and close the business meeting with prayer, which may be offered by the president or one of the other officers or by the superintendent.

The Children's Responsibility for the Business.—Give the children as much responsibility for the business of the society as possible. Let them learn, while they are boys and girls, that every church has to conduct its affairs in a businesslike way if it would prosper, and that it is serving the Lord to do his work efficiently and wisely. Talk with the children about some of the business that comes before church officers and the questions they have to decide. Let the children themselves conduct as much of the business as possible, rehearsing them beforehand, if need be, in order that the meeting may be conducted in an orderly manner. Let the secretary read the names of the new members who have been approved by the superintendent for active membership. Sometimes let the Juniors propose new measures that are to be discussed in the meeting, and try so far as possible to teach the Juniors to carry on a business meeting themselves, as a church business meeting is carried on, or as a church business meeting should be carried on.

The superintendent should be behind all this business meeting, and should guide it, but should teach the children to do it, with proper guidance, and, while keeping a hand on the reins, should so far as possible keep in the background, that the children may learn to depend upon themselves and to do business wisely.

Questions for Review.

(*a*) How often shall business meetings be held?
(*b*) Shall they be held in connection with the prayer-meetings?
(*c*) What business should be transacted at these meetings?
(*d*) Who shall preside?
(*e*) How much responsibility shall the children have for the business of the society?

CHAPTER XII.

Junior Executive Committee.—The Junior executive committee, like the executive committee of the Young People's society, should consist of the officers of the society and of the chairmen of the different committees. They are really the mainspring of the society, and should be very carefully chosen. It should consist of the most responsible and reliable boys and girls in the society, and much should be intrusted to them.

How Often to Meet.—This committee should meet, if possible, once a month. Junior superintendents are usually very busy people, with more of other kinds of Christian work on their shoulders than ought to be there; properly to conduct a Junior Endeavor society gives scope for all the abilities of one person without expecting other church-work from her. However, it usually happens that they are also Sunday-school teachers, and perhaps are doing much other work in the church; and it may not be always possible for them to hold these meetings of the Junior executive committee as often as once a month.

It certainly should not be less often than once in two months, and it might perhaps alternate with the regular business meetings of the society, letting the executive committee hold a meeting with the superin-

tendent once a month, and the next month holding
the regular business meeting with the society. These
meetings should be carefully planned beforehand, that
they may be of real benefit to those who shall take
part in them, and a real help to the society. If the
superintendent can invite the members of this committee to her own house to tea, and after a little social
time with them take up the business to be conducted,
she will find herself becoming much better acquainted
with the children than she can become in any number
of meetings, and will hear much about their school and
home life as they chatter together in this social way;
and this will help her to understand them and know
how to help them.

Plan for a Large Society.—Where a society is
large and there are many committees, the executive
committee may be so large that it is not easy to do
this; but in such a case it may be wise to let the
executive committee consist only of the officers, and
to invite to its meetings one or two chairmen of committees each time, until every chairman has been invited once. In a small society, however, which has
only four or five committees, these chairmen should be
considered as belonging regularly to the executive
committee, as in the older society.

How to Conduct the Meeting.—These meetings
should be conducted as are those of the Young People's
society. Let the officers and the chairmen of committees plan for these meetings beforehand, always
watching the society meetings to see what topics they
think need to be discussed.

Let the superintendent also be on the watch, and let

her bring before this committee some of the questions that perplex her in her guidance of the society as she can wisely present these to them.   So far as possible, take these boys and girls into your confidence. Help them to feel that it is their society, not yours alone, and that they as well as you are responsible for the guidance of it.   Bring up questions of finance, of good order, of winning new members, of helping all the members to greater faithfulness; questions of their relation to the church as a society.

Let the boys and girls themselves suggest ways of helping the church and the pastor and the Sunday-school. Help them to feel their responsibility as leaders in keeping up the tone of the society and in making it felt in the day-school.   In short, let them be to the society in a small degree, and as children may, something of what the " pillars of the church " are to that organization and to their pastor.   If you take this attitude with them, you will find it possible in time to lean upon these boys and girls as a real help in the administration of the society ; and they in their turn will learn to be efficient Christian workers, and to take their part in the life and business of the church when they are older.

Who Should Preside.—Let the Junior president preside at these meetings of the executive committee, and let him conduct them as nearly as possible as the same meetings are conducted by the Young People's society. It would be a help to him if the president of the Young People's society would invite him occasionally to one of the meetings of the executive committee of the older society, and perhaps have some subject that is common to both societies discussed at such a meeting.

Many questions can be frankly talked over at these little cabinet meetings that cannot wisely be brought before the whole society; and, if you trust the boys and girls, you will find that they *can* be trusted. Teach the president how to preside at these meetings, and let him learn here how to preside, that he may not need to lean at all upon the superintendent at the business meetings of the society, but may be able to do his work promptly and efficiently at those meetings.

The Secretary's Part.—Let the secretary record the business transacted and the questions discussed at these meetings, and always at the meeting of the executive committee read a report of the last meeting. As has been said, there will sometimes be consultations and discussions at these meetings that could not wisely be considered in the general business meetings of the society, and sometimes there will be measures discussed here that had better not be reported to the society in general; but occasionally, at least, the secretary should report these meetings to the society, that all the boys and girls may know that these meetings are held, and that they have much to do with the welfare of the society.

Make these little cabinet meetings a real power in the society, and put into them so much study and thought that they will really be of value to those who attend them. Study also to make them pleasant to the boys and girls who come, and make them opportunities for getting closer to these Junior officers and committees, nearer to their hearts, and better informed as to their every-day lives and the influence of the society upon their conduct.

The Greatest Value of These Meetings.—Perhaps the greatest value of these little meetings is in the opportunity they give to the superintendent for an intimate acquaintance and real friendship with these boys and girls, and the possibilities of giving them larger help than could be given if they were seen only in the meetings and sociables of the society. Sometimes, too, invite the pastor to these meetings, and let the Junior president ask him to preside and to say to these leaders among the boys and girls some of the things that he would sometimes like to say to them, and to give them counsel and encouragement, and let it also help them to a sense of comradeship, not only with their superintendent, but also with their pastor in their work for Christ and his church.

Questions for Review.

(*a*) How shall the Junior executive committee be constituted?

(*b*) How often shall this committee meet?

(*c*) How shall these meetings be conducted?

(*d*) Who shall preside?

(*e*) Shall the secretary report these meetings to the society?

CHAPTER XIII.

The Number of Committees.—There should be in each Junior Endeavor society just as many committees as are necessary in order to do the work committed to that society, and no more. Every active member of the society should be placed on some committee, and should be given some work to do, and should also be taught how to do it. The number of active members will therefore be an indication of the number of committees required in a society. As a rule there should be at least four or five members on each committee, though if the society is very small three committee members will have to be enough; but it is better to have a few committees, with members enough on each to do the work well, than to multiply the committees. The children should be taught that in doing this committee work they are really doing something for Christ and the church, and that they can best please Jesus by doing thorough work.

Committee Work for Preparatory Members.—There should also be some work found for the preparatory members to do, though of course none of the very important work should be given to them.

Some societies try the plan of putting all the boys who are in the preparatory membership on a Band of Mercy committee with an active member as chairman,

and all the preparatory members who are girls on a
"helping-hand committee," with an active member
also for their chairman, making it their work to help
the sunshine committee whenever their help is needed.
But, whatever committees may be used, let the
thought always be kept before the children that *love*
to Christ means *service* for Christ, and all this committee work is only one way of showing our love
to him by doing something to help in the work of the
church.

The Most Necessary Committees.—As has already been said, each society should use such committees as are necessary to keep all the members of the
society at work; but some committees are more
important than others, and two or three are *necessary*
to the work of the society, and should be appointed
even if the society is so small that only one can be on
each committee. Every society, however small its
membership, should have a lookout committee and a
prayer-meeting committee, and if possible a missionary
committee: a lookout committee to keep its own
membership faithful and to help to secure new
members for the society; the prayer-meeting committee to do all they can to help make the prayer-
meetings what they should be; and a missionary committee to remind them that they must reach out
beyond their own borders, and do all they can to help
win the world to Christ.

It is difficult to say just which is the most important committee, though in general these three might
be considered such, in the order named; but each
child should be taught to consider his own committee

the most important one for him, since that is the work committed to him to do, and that society is the best whose members are most faithful in keeping their pledge and in doing the work assigned to them.

How to Appoint the Committees.—The chairmen of these committees should usually be appointed by the superintendent. The other members of each committee might be chosen by the chairmen, consulting together with the superintendent, referring always to the superintendent for final decision in case it should happen that the same person should be chosen for two committees. In general it is wise to put those children on the same committee who will be likely to do the best work with one another and with the chairman of that committee, and so far as possible regard should be had to their own preferences in regard to the kind of work they shall do and the children they shall work with. Care should be taken, however, from year to year, that the children may work on several different committees in the course of their four or five years or more of membership in the Junior society, that they may learn how to do different kinds of work.

Varieties of Committee Work.—These committees can all be trained to do real work, and work that is worth doing; but it will necessitate much time and thought on the part of the superintendent or her helpers. In the following chapters certain definite plans of work will be suggested that can be adopted by different committees, and a wise and resourceful superintendent will be able of herself to suggest many variations and adaptations of these plans. What is suggested here is meant simply to show samples of work that has been done or that might be done by Junior committees ; but it is not necessary that any two societies should do their work in exactly the same way, or that any of these suggestions should be followed exactly as they are given, unless they are found just suitable for any society that may wish to try them.

Who Should Direct the Committees.—All the committee work should be under the general supervision and direction of the superintendent, but she should delegate the larger part of it to the Junior committee chosen from the older society to help her in her work. If there is no such committee in the older society, there should be one appointed if possible. Where this cannot be done, the superintendent should feel the care of the work, giving as much of the detail as possible to the older Juniors. If there are two or three assistants, each one should have certain committees assigned to her, and should plan the work with the Juniors themselves.

Varieties of Work for Juniors.—Many Juniors have already done much work for Christ and the church through these committees, and any superintendent who would like to know just what they are doing will find many samples of their work described in each number of *The Christian Endeavor World* and in *The Junior Christian Endeavor World.* Of course the work always varies with the different surroundings and possibilities of the different societies ; but it has been found that some very small societies and with many difficulties in their way have done very faithful work, and have set an example that might well be followed by societies that are accomplishing less with larger opportunities.

As examples of some of the different kinds of work that Juniors have done let me copy here a few extracts from a report given by a Junior superintendent of one of the Provinces in Canada, telling of work that had been done by the Juniors of one province alone. She reports thirty-eight Junior societies with a membership of about one thousand. She says: " We are able to report societies helping to pay church debts, making scrap-books for the sick and shut-ins, dressing dolls for Christmas trees, sending papers to the Northwest and flowers to the sick in hospitals. One society furnished a cot in the hospital, and each week one or two of the committee visited the cot with something to please the sick children. Another provided fruit, vegetables, cake, etc., for the Old Folks' Home. Even our sailor friends were not forgotten, one society having made eighteen sailor bags and filled them for the sailors.

" Some of the flower committees have taken bouquets of flowers to the French missionary, who gives them to the sailors on the boats he meets. A card is attached, on which is written a verse of Scripture,—in French on one side and English on the other,—which is reported to be very much appreciated by the sailors. One society has sent away over six hundred pages of literature to lumber camps. Another society reports that nine boys made sixteen scrap-books and filled fifty marble-bags out of their own money. Some of our societies are taking up a systematic course of

Bible-study, and, while most limit themselves to the topic books, one superintendent reports a departure. He says, ' We have taken up the " Pilgrim's Progress " in the meeting, selecting the topics and references, and basing the talk (with blackboard illustrations) on the incidents of Pilgrim's journey. It proved very interesting.' These are only a few of the many good things that our Junior work has accomplished."

If Juniors from one Province have accomplished all this, it is plain that the united efforts of our boys and girls the world around will result in great good.

Questions for Review.

(*a*)   How many committees may there be in a society?
(*b*)   What committees are *necessary* ?
(*c*)   What are the most important committees ?
(*d*)   Who shall select the members of committees ?
(*e*)   What real work can these committees do ?
(*f*)   Who shall direct and plan this work ?
(*g*)   Are any Juniors now doing real work for Christ through these committees ?

CHAPTER XIV.

THE LOOKOUT COMMITTEE.

How Chosen.—Since the lookout committee is one of the most important of all the committees, it should be very carefully selected. The superintendent herself should choose the chairman from among the older members, trying to find some one who is an earnest Christian boy or girl, and also one whose religion commends itself to the other children. The chairman of the lookout committee ought to be as wise and winsome a Christian as can be found among the active members, some one who will really try to help the other boys and girls to be faithful, and will do it in a pleasant way. If you cannot find a perfect saint among your boys and girls, take an imperfect one, and help him to feel that, if he is not a saint, he is called to be one and to help others to be saints, too.

The superintendent should also keep in close touch with the chairman of the lookout committee, and should talk the work over with him carefully and prayerfully, both before he begins it and as often as possible in the course of the year. If you have chosen your chairman wisely, he may safely be trusted to choose others who shall work with him on the committee, for the boys and girls know one another as well as any older friend can know them. As has been said before, the different chairmen of committees can, if thought best, hold a meeting with their superintendent, and choose their helpers together.   It should always be understood, however, that the superintendent has a controlling voice in deciding on which committee each boy or girl shall work.

Getting New Members.—A part of the work of the lookout committee as given in the constitution of the Junior Society is to help secure new members for the society.   It cannot, of course, be left to the children to decide who shall become members; but they can help by inviting other children to the meetings and by telling the superintendent of certain boys and girls they know who seem to them ready to become active members.   In every society the rule should be that a boy or a girl must on first entering the society become a preparatory member for a time, till the superintendent has had a chance to judge of his fitness; but any children may be invited to come to the meetings, even if they are not yet ready to become members; and here the lookout committee can do good work by inviting children to come, and by waiting for them after school, or by calling at their homes and walking to the meeting with them when they go for the first time.   It is quite possible, too, that the members of the lookout committee may know of some child who ought to be asked to become an active member.   In such cases they should mention the names to the superintendent, from whom alone invitations to be active members should be given, and who should so far as possible be assured of the sincerity and earnestness of the child before giving the invitation.

Securing Faithfulness to the Meetings.—Another duty of the lookout committee is to help the other Juniors to greater faithfulness in attending the meetings, and there is much that an earnest lookout committee can do along this line. The chairman of the lookout committee should keep in a little blank book a list of the names of all the members of the society, active and preparatory, and should mark their attendance in her book. Each member of this committee should also be furnished with a little book, and each one should have a certain number of names written, and should keep the record of the attendance in this book.

The lookout committee ought, if possible, to hold a five minutes' committee meeting after each regular meeting of the society, and then, going over their books together, find out what members are absent. The names should be divided among the committee, and each one should be expected to see certain ones and find out the reason of their absence.

If thought best, a little card might be prepared, asking for a written reason for absence, with blanks left to be filled up either by the absent member or by his or her parents. With such a card any member of the lookout committee could easily go to any absent member, and ask to have the blanks filled up; but let the work of the lookout committee be clearly explained to the whole society, so that they will know that these cards are coming, and will be prepared to fill out the blanks if for any reason they are absent.

If a Junior is absent on account of sickness or absence from town, the member of the committee who has his name might write opposite it on his book the word " Excused." If the absence is for any other reason, the superintendent of the society should decide whether or not the absence was excusable; and all of these excuse cards should as often as once a month be handed in to the superintendent, that she may learn easily and quickly just what reasons keep any of her Juniors away from the meetings. She will find on these excuse cards good texts for some of her subsequent talks to the children.

Securing Faithfulness to Bible-Reading and Prayer.—Another duty of the lookout committee should be to do what they can to help the other Juniors to greater faithfulness in keeping their promises in regard to daily Bible-reading and prayer. It might seem at first thought that there is nothing the boys and girls can do in this direction, but that such watchfulness of the children as this should be the duty of the superintendent. Of course all the work of the lookout committee must be done under the supervision of the superintendent or of some older person; but the records can be kept by the lookout committee, and through the superintendent they can keep watch of the work the children are doing.

It is only the active members who take this pledge of Bible-reading and daily prayer, though all the children should be urged to consider this as a part of their daily duty and privilege; but, since the active members are the only ones who are pledged to do it, there will not be so many names to be considered.

A Roll-Call for Bible-Reading.—It might well be the custom that once every month, either at the consecration meeting, or at the monthly business meeting, the roll of the society should be called, and each one should tell just where he is reading in the Bible, and the members of the lookout committee should write it down in their little books opposite the names. A separate place in their books might be kept where the names of the active members are written, and opposite each name the place where he was reading in the Bible at the last roll-call. In this way it is possible to know not only that the boys and girls are reading their Bibles, but also just how they are reading them, and whether they have any definite plan for their reading. This gives an opportunity also for the superintendent to suggest some good plan of Bible-study to those who have none, if they have not been helped in this way at home. In any case, do not let the boys and girls under your care form careless habits in reading their Bibles, if it is possible to help them to something better.

How Juniors May Read the Bible.—For some children it is a good plan to begin their Bibles at the beginning and read them through; for others it is perhaps better to suggest that they begin by reading the New Testament through, or even a single book of the New Testament; others may prefer to read each day the daily readings given in connection with their Sunday-school lessons or their Christian Endeavor topic.

It might be made a part of the work of the prayer-meeting committee or of the lookout committee to write out copies of these suggested readings, and give one to each member for each month. Try to make

sure that none of the Juniors form the careless habit
of opening the Bible to any place where it may happen
to open, and reading hastily a few verses there, with
little or no thought of what they are reading. Such
reading of their Bibles is very little better than no
reading at all.

Try also to form in the children the habit of reading the Bible every morning as well as every evening.
Many children may say that they have not time to
read it in the morning, but it does not take many
minutes to read a single verse, or even two or three
verses; and, if the verse is carefully chosen, and is
thought over a little during the day, it may be a real
help to the child.

Perhaps some children would find it a good plan to
read the suggested Christian Endeavor reading in the
morning, and then read the Bible in course at night.
The reading in connection with the Christian Endeavor topic is usually very short.

Promoting Better Christian Living.—The lookout
committee should also be taught to feel that it is their
duty to do all they can to help the other boys and
girls to greater faithfulness in Christian living. The
boys and girls cannot do this work by preaching; but
in little ways they can make their influence felt, and
they can always feel that they of all members of the
society must be sure to make their example what it
should be. Sometimes, too, it will certainly be possible for them to speak a word to some other boy or
girl that will help him or her to decide for the right.
Each one ought to be able to help his most intimate
friend to right living and right thinking, both by words

and example and by silent influence. Try to help your lookout committee to feel their responsibility in this direction, and to be very much in earnest in doing this. Hold occasional little prayer-meetings just with the lookout committee alone, with this thought of faithfulness among themselves as their theme; and help them also to feel that their faithfulness must show at home.

How Junior Committees May Help.—As has already been said, all this work should be under the general supervision of the superintendent, though, if the society is large, she may not be able to attend to the details of it. If there is a Junior committee, some member of that committee ought to feel it her especial work to attend carefully to all the details of this work, meeting the lookout committee for five minutes after each meeting, and talking with them about the week's work, looking over the list of absentees and their excuses, and keeping careful record herself of their faithfulness in Bible-reading and prayer and in Christian living at home and school and in the society. With careful and prayerful supervision a Junior lookout committee ought to do very good work in the society, and in working for others ought to learn much of the beauty and joy of Christian service and Christian living. Try to accomplish this in your society.

Questions for Review.

(*a*) What children should be chosen for the lookout committee?

(*b*) What can they properly do to secure new members?

(*c*)   How can they help other Juniors to be faithful in attending the meetings?

(*d*)   How can they help them to be faithful in daily prayer and Bible-reading?

(*e*)   Who should direct the work of this committee?

CHAPTER XV.

Choosing the Prayer-Meeting Committee.—The prayer-meeting committee should also be carefully chosen, the chairman being selected by the superintendent, and the other members chosen as may seem best, either by the chairman himself or by the superintendent. They should be among the older members of the society, old enough to feel some responsibility for the prayer-meeting and to know something of their own ability to help make it a good prayer-meeting.

This is one of the committees where boys can be especially useful. In some societies the committee is made up wholly of boys, since there are many things that they can do to help the prayer-meeting, and since it is good for them to feel the responsibility for it. The boys should be taught that they will be expected, when they grow older, to be able to lead a church prayer-meeting and to help in many ways to make the church prayer-meeting what it should be. A boy who learns to take a helpful part in planning and carrying on the prayer-meeting is getting ready to be a helpful member of his church when he is older, and it is good for them to look forward to just such helpfulness in their own church.

The Supervision of This Committee.—The work of this committee should be under the supervision of some member of the Junior committee, who should consult with the superintendent, plan with the committee, and hold occasional little special prayer-meetings with them, and help them to have a high ideal of what a good prayer-meeting is, and to know how to make a prayer-meeting what it should be. A bright, earnest Christian boy can do much for the prayer-meeting, and can help to interest and hold the other boys, if once his own sympathy and interest have been enlisted.

Little Things That Help the Prayer-Meeting.—A wise superintendent will think of many things that this committee can do to help the prayer-meetings. It might well be their duty to arrive five minutes before the meeting begins, and to see that the chairs or settees are properly arranged, and the Bibles and hymn-books ready. If the society is large, they might also help the lookout committee in keeping a record of those who are absent, and in seeing some of the absent ones with the excuse cards spoken of in the preceding chapter.

This prayer-meeting committee, too, can do something to help make the atmosphere right for the meeting by sitting near some of the younger children and helping to keep them quiet. They might also help in seating the late comers if the society is large, and be ready to look after visitors if any such shall come to the meetings.

Sometimes, too, the superintendent may like to have a little of their help in blackboard work before the meeting begins, in writing out questions for her, or, if they are gifted in such work, in drawing illustrations for her talk. This committee might also be appointed to write copies of the prayer-meeting topics to give to each active member, or to write on slips of paper Bible verses that the superintendent may want given out in the meeting.

Helping Bible-Reading Habits.—In some societies it might be a good plan to appoint the prayer-meeting committee to write out beforehand on separate slips of paper copies of the suggested Sunday-school readings or Christian Endeavor readings to give to those active members who are using those topics for their daily Bible-reading. If for a month or a week at a time each active member had such a slip to keep in his Bible, he would be much less likely to forget his Bible-reading, and would be more likely to read regularly and methodically. It is so easy for a boy or a girl to lose the Sunday-school quarterly, or even the Junior topic book, and then get careless in Bible-reading because the topics are lost.

How This Committee Can Help the Meeting.—So far we have been speaking of work that the prayer-meeting committee might do before the meeting begins, either in their own homes or in the prayer-meeting room; but there are many ways in which an earnest prayer-meeting committee may not only prepare beforehand for the prayer-meeting, but may help to make the meeting itself what it should be.

They can do something, at least by their own example, to help keep order in the room. If there are slips or cards to be passed around during the meeting, they can be ready for this service. They can always carefully prepare for their own part in the meeting, and have something helpful to say, and can say it in the beginning of the meeting, while the other members are hesitating as to what to say.

They can also, if the superintendent desires it, take turns in bringing to the meeting some helpful clipping from *The Junior Christian Endeavor World,* or from their missionary magazine, or they can act as an information committee by giving each time one interesting item about some other society.

Definite Work for Each Member.—In a society where the children are young, and have not much to say in the meeting, it might be well to give each member of the prayer-meeting committee something definite to report each time as his part of the meeting. One member might give one helpful thought from the last sermon he heard; another might read one Junior letter from *The Junior Christian Endeavor World;* another might give one item from some other Junior society; and others might give each of them one missionary item. In this way the prayer-meeting committee will always have something interesting and helpful to say.

The members of this committee, too, ought always to be ready to lead in sentence prayers; and they should be asked always to remember to pray for the meeting before they come to it. If the members of this committee are really Christian boys, as of course they should be before they become active members, they will be ready and willing to help in all these ways.

Meetings of This Committee.—It is a good thing for this committee, as for every other, to hold frequent committee meetings under the guidance of the super-intendent or some other older person who has the supervision of their work. These meetings of the prayer-meeting committee can be made very helpful occasions for these boys. When it is possible to do so, it is well to have them in the home of their leader, as has been suggested concerning other committees, that she may make it more of a social occasion and an opportunity for getting better acquainted with them than is possible in the larger meetings of the society, or even in a small committee meeting if it is held in the church. The children greatly appreciate such invitations, and it ought to be possible for most Junior workers to give them at least occasionally.

Advantages of a Home Gathering.—In such a social home gathering it is possible to take time for a quiet, reverent prayer-meeting with the boys, in which they shall carefully and prayerfully plan their work for the next month, talking over the work they have tried to do, or failed to do, or neglected to do, and pray for help for more earnest, more willing, and more efficient service in the coming month. In such a quiet little meeting as this, with four or five boys alone, their superintendent ought to be able to get very near to their hearts, and to strengthen her own influence and the influence of the society upon them, and to stimu-late them to larger and better work for the society.

If this earnest little prayer-meeting can be followed by a little supper, or by light refreshments of some kind, and then by a pleasant social time, it will leave a doubly pleasant impression on their minds, and will be found very helpful.

Some Shorter Committee Meetings.—But children are many, and workers are few, and of course it is not always possible to hold such gatherings as this; yet our boys must have their committee meetings. Let it, then, be the custom to hold a five-minute committee meeting after each prayer-meeting or before it, and at least as often as once a month make it a fifteen-minute meeting. At such meetings it is possible to have reports of the work they have been doing, and to assign to each his work for the next month, and to have suggestions for the improvement of the prayer-meetings and prayers for the members. It might be well sometimes to let the boys tell you of anything they noticed in the last prayer-meeting that was not as it should be, and ask what they think could be done to remedy such defects. Help them in every way to feel that the prayer meeting is their special care, and that they are to think of it and to watch it, not to criticise, but to help improve it.

Sometimes, too, have a special little prayer-meeting with this committee just before the regular meeting of the society, to pray for the meeting and for all who shall attend it.

Flexibility Possible.—Many suggestions have been given in this chapter, and it may sound to some who read this as if too much were being asked of its members, and too many plans were proposed; but of course each society is to adopt only such suggestions as will be found really helpful in that society. A large society may find it possible and necessary to try many of these methods, while a smaller one, whose members live far apart, can try only one or two. Try any plans or variations of them that seem helpful to you for your society, and no others; only try in some way to make this committee feel that the prayer-meeting is theirs and that they are to help it in every possible way.

Questions for Review.

(*a*)   Who should be chosen for this committee?
(*b*)   Who shall direct their work?
(*c*)   What work can they do before the meeting?
(*d*)   Prayer-meetings for the prayer-meeting committee:
  how often? how long? when?

CHAPTER XVI.

The Importance of This Work.—One of the most important parts of the work of the Junior Endeavor society is the training given to the children in missionary work. Every member who graduates from the Junior society should have some education in missions; and more, perhaps, than many of the older members of the church have to-day. They ought to learn in the Junior society not only to be interested in missions, but to have an intelligent knowledge of the work of their own board, and of their own duty towards missionary work. This education should be given them by frequent missionary meetings and by various methods of work for missions that can be carried on through the missionary committee.

Systematic and Proportionate Giving for Children.—A proper training in missionary work means first of all that the children should be trained to generous, systematic, and proportionate giving. Too many children give simply the money that their mothers have put into their hands to give, with very little thought about it. It cannot be really generous giving, so far as they themselves are concerned, unless they give something that is their own, and give it because they really want to help to extend Christ's kingdom in the world.

At least once in every year there ought to be a

Junior meeting devoted to this subject of giving, in which the different ways of giving should be carefully explained, and the boys and girls should be helped to see very plainly what Jesus would like to have them do; and the first thing he wants is that they should give generously and heartily of what is their own. The gift may be small, and yet it may be a generous one, if it is the child's own, and is given in the right spirit.

They should be taught, also, to have some system and proportion in their giving. The natural impulse of the human heart, old or young, seems to be to give to whatever object happens especially to interest the giver; and to a certain extent this impulse is a right one, and should be yielded to; but, if every Christian gave in this way and only in this way, there would probably be plenty of money for orphans and for fresh air, and perhaps for medical missionaries and city missions; but it would be hard to find the money for plain, every-day mission work, and to erect and keep in repair suitable buildings, and to provide for touring and much of the routine of mission work, which must be provided for, but does not sound so romantic or interesting.

Interest in the Church Boards to be Cultivated.— Every Christian ought to feel that he has a certain part of the responsibility for the work of his own boards, home and foreign, and he ought to feel just as anxious to do his part, so far as he is able, in keeping the missionary treasury free from debt as to keep his own private treasury provided for. A debt of his missionary board is his debt, and he should feel it so, and his boys and girls should be taught to feel it so.

In planning their benevolence each year they should always plan to give a certain definite proportion of their money to the regular work of their own boards, reserving whatever proportion seems right for special causes that may appeal to them from time to time. Help the boys and girls to have a system in their giving, and the benevolence of future years will not be so spasmodic and haphazard as much of the giving of these latter years has been.

Education in Denominational Missions.—A good way to introduce the children to their missionary boards is to devote one prayer-meeting to that subject. Explain to them the organization of the boards, the field for which they are working, the number of workers they are employing, the yearly expense of the various missions, the sources from which the boards obtain the money to support all this work, and the responsibility of each church-member to help support this work. Tell them something of the history of their own board, and the motive which leads to all the work, until all this organized missionary work seems very clear to them, and they see plainly their own relation to the board.

All this sounds rather dry, perhaps, told so concisely ; but the meeting may be made one of the most interesting of the year if you make it sufficiently realistic. Illustrate the meeting with maps and diagrams, and pieces of money ; and put stickers on your map, or have some imaginary secretaries of the board visit your society and tell of their work ; or draw a tree, and let the trunk of the tree represent the board, and the branches and twigs the churches and individual members of the churches. Consecrated ingenuity will find many ways of illustrating this meeting so as to make it intensely interesting.

How Gifts May be Divided.—A plan that has been tried in some societies, and has been found helpful, is to divide into three parts all the money to be given away, giving one-third directly to the pledged work of the foreign missionary board, to be used for the regular work of the board, another third in the same way to the home missionary board, and using the last third for special gifts in our own land or other lands, which may enlist our sympathies, making the general division of the whole amount such that about half is spent in our own country and the other half in other lands.

Such a division as this allows an opportunity to help Armenian or Hindoo orphans, or to make special gifts to missionaries, to fresh-air funds, or city missions, and similar causes that are always needing our help, and are always of interest, partly because they seem more tangible. If *this plan* does not commend itself to you, try some other; but *have a plan* for your giving, and have some principle about it; and do not let the boys and girls grow up with the habit of giving only by impulse to the cause which for the moment interests them most.

Missionary Meetings: How Often.—Each Junior society must decide for itself how often a missionary meeting should be held; but, since our whole aim as Christian Endeavorers is to first give our own selves to the Lord, and then to lead to him as many others as possible, it would seem that the missionary work should have a large place in our thoughts and our prayers. Many societies think it best to have a missionary meeting once every month, and others once in two or three months, having a regular day for it, so that the children may know just when to expect it, and taking such pains to make the meetings vivid and interesting that those meetings are the most attractive of the month.

It is needless to say that the societies that do this are the ones that arouse the most interest in missions, and that, according to their means, give the most largely. The society that has only occasional missionary meetings, and does not take much pains with those, cannot expect to have much interest in missions. But in these days, when material for missionary meetings is so plentiful, a dull missionary meeting ought to be an impossibility for any live Junior society.

How to Conduct Them.—The missionary meetings will naturally be conducted a little differently from the other meetings, and the children can take a larger part in them. It affords an opportunity, too, to let an occasional preparatory member take part in the meeting. Let a member of the missionary committee lead the missionary meeting, and let the members of the society take charge of the whole meeting. The superintendent should help them plan it; but, when it is planned, just as much of the carrying out of these plans as possible should be left to the children.

Sometimes let the children imagine themselves missionaries from different lands, and tell the story of their work. Sometimes hold a missionary convention, or an annual mission meeting, letting the children imagine themselves members of the mission, while they tell of their work of last year and their plans for next year.

Sometimes have some little foreign guests at your meeting, letting some of the Juniors make believe that they are Chinese boys and girls, some of them from mission schools or hospitals, and others from heathen homes, and let them tell the story of their lives.

Different Plans.—Sometimes have a biographical missionary meeting, having Livingstone and Moffat and Carey and Judson and others come to your meeting in the forms of some of your brightest Juniors. Sometimes make a missionary journey, visiting some special missionary in whom you want to interest your Juniors, or visiting just one city, and finding out just how many missionaries are there and what they are all doing. Material for such meetings can be found in almost any missionary magazines, by rewriting in the first person and simplifying some of the missionary letters, and also in the numerous missionary libraries. Your own missionary board can probably also send interesting material for a few cents. Home missionary meetings can also be planned in the same way.

The Work of the Missionary Committee.—It should be the work of the missionary committee to plan with their superintendent the missionary meetings and to help carry out these plans, to prepare with the help of the superintendent or some member of the Junior committee a card for each member of the society, on which shall be written the name of one missionary whom he is requested to adopt for his own missionary, to pray for every day, and to become acquainted with through the missionary magazines. A pretty missionary picture pasted on this card will add to its attractiveness, and make it more probable that it will be preserved and the missionary remembered. The committee might well be recognized by the church as a part of the missionary work of the church, and in some churches it might be possible once in a while to give the Juniors a part in the monthly missionary meeting of the church. The superintendent should try, also, to keep this committee in touch with the other missionary organizations of the church so far as possible, that the whole church may be working together for missions.

Questions for Review.

(*a*)   How shall the children be educated in missions ?

(*b*)   How shall they be trained to generous, systematic, and proportionate giving ?

(*c*)   How shall the children become acquainted with their missionary boards ?

(*d*)   How shall they divide their money for benevolences ?

(*e*)   How often should a missionary meeting be held ?

(*f*)   How shall the missionary meetings be conducted ?

CHAPTER XVII.

A Committee for the Younger Children.—The sunshine committee seems to be pre-eminently the *children's* committee, and some of the younger Juniors can be assigned to it, with one older Junior as chairman and some older person to supervise their work. The superintendent should always be ready to suggest work to this committee; but some member of the Junior committee ought to be prepared to carry out these plans, since so many cares must of necessity come upon the superintendent.

The work of this committee varies very much according to the community in which the children live, and the needs of their own church and of their neighbors'. In general, their work is to put as much brightness into the lives of other people as they can, and to be sunny, happy little Christians themselves. Just how they shall " make sunshine" they must decide for themselves; but any bright, earnest little Juniors will find plenty of ways to do it and plenty of places where more sunshine is needed.

Sunshine at Home.—The very first place where each member of this committee should begin to make sunshine is in her own home. The superintendent should hold a little meeting with this committee alone, at the beginning of the year, talking with them very simply about their work, and helping them to see that sunshine, like charity, " must begin at home," and not end there. Let the children themselves tell of some ways in which they can make their own homes brighter and happier.

Ask whether they ever make clouds and darkness in the homes, and what kind of words and deeds make these clouds. Ask them to pray every day that God will make them sunny-hearted and glad to look at the bright side of things. Give each one a little sunshine card to keep at home, and let her mark it with a cross or a circle, according to her own judgment as to whether she has or has not really tried to be kind and unselfish and thoughtful for others in her own home. If she thinks at night that she has not tried very much, ask her to tell her Father in heaven that she is sorry and to pray for strength and willingness to do better the next day.

A sunshine committee that is worthy of its name ought to make itself felt at home. It might be a good plan to send a card to the mother of each member of the sunshine committee, telling her that her child is appointed to the sunshine committee and that the first duty of this committee is to make sunshine at home, and asking the mother to help her child in doing this and to suggest ways of doing it.

Sunshine at School.—Another place which this committee can brighten is the Sunday-school and day-school. Some children are anything but sunbeams to their Sunday-school and day-school teachers ; but the members of this committee must feel it their duty to keep the shadows off as much as possible and to do what they can, by quiet attention and a knowledge of their lessons, to put brightness into the work of these teachers, who are trying to do so much for them.

A member of the sunshine committee should feel that by abstaining so far as possible from whispering, and by sitting quietly in her place and listening when her teacher talks, and being ready to answer any question asked her, she can brighten her Sunday-school teacher's work. Such an example will do something towards helping other children to be more quiet and attentive, too, though, alas! good examples are not always followed even by older people.

In day-school, too, there are endless opportunities for the sunshine children to help by their words and their example, and by kindness and unselfishness in their play, and by a general spirit of helpfulness. It would not hurt the day-school teacher to be informed that certain children are on the Junior sunshine committee, and that, if she will show them how, they really do want to make a little sunshine in school.

Sunshine for the Aged.—These little sunbeams can do something, too, to make life brighter for the old people in the church and for invalids and shut-ins. Sometimes a birthday card or an Easter or Christmas card sent to some invalid or aged person will brighten a lonely life. Sometimes it may be a little bouquet of wild flowers brought in from the woods, and sometimes flowers from the child's own garden ; sometimes a little call made by the whole committee, if the superintendent feels sure that it would be welcomed. Some Juniors have once in the year given a sociable to the old people of the church, and have entertained them in so bright and beautiful a way that it has made a very happy occasion for those who greatly appreciate such little kindnesses. Teach the Juniors first of all to honor the grandparents in their own homes, and brighten their lives, and then to help carry happiness to other aged people.

Sunshine for the Sick.—Often, too, there are invalids who are very grateful for some little attention that the children can show to them. The days go slowly and wearily by to those who must spend their time in a sick-room, and something that pleasantly breaks the monotony comes like a ray of real sunshine. Let the Juniors find out who in the community is sick, and occasionally send flowers or some little delicacy, and, if thought best, go once in a while to call on the invalid, and perhaps to sing one of their little songs, if desired. Always, however, before such visits are made the superintendent should find out whether they would be acceptable, that the children may go only to those places where their presence would really carry sunshine.

Sometimes this sunshine committee might visit the hospital if there is one near them, and sing songs and leave flowers for those who care for them. In their own committee meetings they might prepare scrap books, dress dolls, or make birthday or Easter or Christmas cards, for those children in the hospital who are well enough to care for such things. Let them think of anything that would amuse them if they were shut up in a hospital, and then prepare such things for the children there.

Sunshine for the Missionaries.—This committee

can also do something to put brightness into missionary lives. They can send a pretty calendar, or a hand-
kerchief, or a bit of ribbon, or some small book, or
other little gift to some missionary as a reminder of
their interest in her. It might be a good plan for them
to celebrate their own birthdays by giving a birthday
gift to the missionary in whom they are most interested. They might also collect and prepare bright
cards to be sent to missionaries to be used for Sunday-
schools and reward cards. Every missionary can use
an unlimited amount of such picture cards for rewards
for the children in her field, and they will all be glad
to get them.

Advertisement cards can be prepared by pasting
white paper over the back of each card, so that the
missionary may write a verse there in the language of
the people she works for. Any pretty bright-colored
picture may be mounted on cardboard and used in this
way, and every sunshine committee can find an unlimited amount of work of this kind. This committee, if
it is composed of girls, can also do some missionary
sewing.

In India some missionaries are glad to get bright-
colored bags made of cretonne or gingham for the
school girls; and missionary magazines will tell of
other wants, some of which this committee ought to
be able to supply.

There is also plenty of opportunity for the children
to do this kind of work for home missionaries and so
put some brightness into their lives. Ask the Ladies'
Aid Society whether they are working for some
home missionary; and, if so, let the sunshine commit-

tee tuck at least one little package into the home missionary barrel.

Sunshine for the Pastor.—There are some things, too, that this committee can do for their church and their pastor. Let them remember their pastor's birthday with some little gift if they will, or at least with a birthday card, and perhaps a birthday letter to which each member of the committee will sign her name. Some birthday committees have a habit of sending an occasional little note to be laid on the pulpit for the pastor to find on Sunday morning, containing just a Bible verse that they think he will like, or a line or two from some sweet poem, with loving greetings from the sunshine committee. Sometimes they might send just a tiny bouquet of bright-colored flowers in a little vase of their own, just for him, from his "sunbeams." Let them in some way remember the pastor's wife when her birthday comes, if it is only with a card or some flowers; anything that shows the pastor or his wife that the children love them, and want to give them a little sunshine, will please them; for it is love that makes sunshine every time.

Sunshine for the Church.—There are little errands, too, that this committee may do for the church, and little services that they may render if they are on the watch for opportunities. In short, there is no limit to the possibilities of a happy, merry, little group of five children, who really are trying to make life brighter for those around them. Try any or all of these plans as you have opportunities, or make other plans of your own; but in some way help the children who are on this committee to let their light shine.

Questions for Review.

(*a*) What is the work of this committee, and who shall direct it?

(*b*) What can the members of this committee do at home?

(*c*) What can they do in the day-school and Sunday-school?

(*d*) What can they do for the old people of the church?

(*e*) What for invalids? for hospitals? for missions?

(*f*) What can they do for their pastor and their church?

CHAPTER XVIII.

Number of Committees.—Besides the committees mentioned in the preceding chapters a Junior society should use as many other committees as may be needed in order that the society may do its best work. Some societies will need a great many committees, and others perhaps only two or three, and even then a very small society may be able to have only one or two members on each committee. Let each society consider carefully just what work it ought to do, and then appoint just the committees necessary to do that, and no more.

Object of Committee Work.—Every active member should be placed on some committee; so the number of active members in a society will help to determine the number of committees needed by that society. The Juniors should be taught from the very beginning of their Christian lives that love for Christ means also service for Christ; that is what all our committees are for, and that is why each active member must be placed upon some committee, that he may be doing some definite work for Christ and the church; and they should be taught to believe that all this committee work should be done heartily, as unto the Lord.

Work for Preparatory Members.—There should

132

also be some work provided for the preparatory members, in the hope that, as they begin to work for Christ they may begin to love him, and may through the way of service come to him. Of course these preparatory members, who are not yet ready to call themselves Christians, cannot be trusted with such work as that done by the lookout and prayer-meeting committees, but there is other work that they can do. All the boys who are preparatory members might, if it were thought best, be placed upon a Band-of-Mercy committee, with an active member as chairman ; and it should be their work to take thoughtful care of their own pets at home, and so far as possible to remind their neighbors to do the same. It should also be their work to protect the squirrels and birds in their neighborhood from those who might be tempted to throw stones at them, or frighten them, or rob their nests. They might also learn how to draw birds around their homes in summer by planting wild berries or something of the sort, and in winter by putting out little food-boxes in the trees, and in summer by keeping a pan of water where the birds can bathe.

Band-of-Mercy Committee.—They should also be careful always to be kind to stray dogs and cats and to every animal, and by their example and their words should do all they can to protect all animals. Teach them that "mercy" means gentleness and kindness to the weak, and since they are the Band of Mercy they will not willingly see any creature more helpless than themselves in any suffering that they can prevent, and that they will also protect little boys and girls if they see them teased by older ones. Occasionally this committee might take the whole charge of a Band-of-Mercy meeting and do what they can to interest the whole society in this work.

Helping-Hand Committee.—The girls who are preparatory members might all be placed on a helping-hand committee, or a whatsoever committee, with an active member for chairman; and it might be their work to help any other committee which especially needs their help. Sometimes they could help the music committee in preparing a song for some special occasion; sometimes they might help the missionary committee in preparing missionary cards or cutting out missionary pictures for a scrap-book. Sometimes they might help the sunshine committee when they are in any special haste in getting ready for Easter or Christmas or some special work. Let this committee become a real help to the society, and teach the committee that in doing this they are really working for Christ and his church.

Music Committee.—The work of the music committee is to make the music as good as possible in every meeting, and to provide special music for special occasions whenever it is needed. This committee might organize a Junior choir, which could lead the singing at every meeting, and could be ready to sing at any Sunday-school concert if the superintendent should desire it. Sometimes in a sociable this committee might have some special music prepared.

The Junior Choir.—It should be the business of this committee to know how many of the Juniors play on the piano or any other instrument, and which ones are the best singers; and it might be well to have

some special music at each sociable. Sometimes a
musical charade or the game of magic music might
be planned for a sociable; and, if the Juniors give an
annual entertainment, or celebrate their anniversary
every year, they might provide special music for that
occasion. In some societies, too, it might be possible
for the music committee to arrange to go occasionally
to some hospital or almshouse to sing for the inmates.
The music committee might also choose a memory
hymn for the society to learn each month, that the
children may keep in their memories some of the
grand old hymns of the church, such as " Nearer, my
God, to thee," " Rock of Ages," and others. Probably there are very few older people who could recite
all the verses of even such a familiar hymn as " Rock
of Ages"; and there are not many, old or young,
that can sing all the verses of " America" without a
book. Let the music committee do what it can to
remedy this state of affairs in the future.

Social Committee.—The social committee should
provide for occasional sociables as frequently as the
superintendent deems wise. These sociables might be
held on a week-day afternoon after school, that the
children may not be kept out in the evening. Indeed,
for the younger Juniors these sociables ought always
to be in the afternoon, and usually for the older ones,
too, though these latter might perhaps have one or two
evening sociables in the course of the year if their
parents approve.

These sociables should be made happy occasions for
the boys and girls; but they should be orderly, and
only such games and amusements should be allowed

as would be approved of by their parents and by the church. Do not let them be occasions for romping or rudeness, though even the best of children may be inclined to be a little too hilarious when a crowd of them are gathered together for a good time. Have a carefully prepared programme for each sociable, making it suitable for the place where it is to be held. Sometimes what might be properly allowed in a home ought not to be allowed in a church. Help the children to have just as good a time as possible, and show them how to have the right kind of good time.

Sociables.—Make your social times opportunities to get better acquainted with the children, for on these occasions you look at them from a different angle, and perhaps see a different side of their character. They will get better acquainted with their superintendent, too; and such opportunities rightly used may help all to better work afterwards in the meetings. Allow at these socials any innocent games that are not too boisterous. Sometimes have an open-air social, and sometimes, if possible, a picnic. Perhaps some societies can occasionally make a trip together in the electric cars, and so have a trolley social, and in country societies it might be possible sometimes to have a sleigh-ride social. It is always helpful to have a carefully prepared programme for these occasions, knowing just what games and amusements will be allowed, that there may be no waiting at the time.

Musical and Literary Sociables.—Sometimes it is well in these sociables to let the first half-hour be given up to musical and literary exercises by the children, letting those who take music lessons play the last pieces of music they learned. Sometimes a very little child might play the prettiest exercise he knows, and another little one might sing, and perhaps an older one might play something on the violin. Then there might be readings and recitations by the children, letting them recite some " memory gem " that they have learned in school. Then after this half-hour the rest of the time might be given to charades or shadow pictures or simple games.

Missionary Socials.—Sometimes have a missionary social, letting the missionary committee help the social committee to prepare it and letting the children all acquire a little new missionary information while they are having a good time.

Temperance Committee.—The temperance committee should do all they can for the cause of temperance. With the help of the superintendent they should plan an occasional temperance meeting, and should, if thought best, circulate temperance pledges among the members, which the boys and girls should take home to show to their parents before they sign them. If thought best these pledges might be " till the signer is twenty-one years old," for some would perhaps sign the pledge for that length of time who would not be willing to sign it for their whole lives. But it is quite probable that a boy who will sign and keep the pledge till he is twenty-one will then be ready to hold to it for the rest of his life. Keep the Juniors informed through this committee of the work of the Woman's Christian Temperance Union and other temperance organizations, and of the temperance laws in their own State and city, and let them sometimes take a vote by ballot on what they think the law should be in their own State or city.

Unusual Committees.—Some societies in exceptional circumstances make use of many other committees, some of them being quite unusual ones. For instance, I have heard of a laundry committee in Japan, and of a peace committee in China, and of a cutting-hair committee and a harmony committee, and visiting committees and relief committees in other lands. Invent your own committees if you can find a use for any kind of Christian work that can better be described by some name that has not been used here; but remember always that the object of all this committee work is to set the children at work for Christ, and to help them always to show their love for Christ by service for him.

Questions for Review.

(*a*)   What other committees might be used in a society if desired?

(*b*)   How many of the active members should be placed on committees?

(*c*)   What work can the preparatory members do?

(*d*)   What is the work of the music committee?

(*e*)   The social committee?

(*f*)   The Band-of-Mercy and temperance committees?

(*g*)   What are some unusual committees that have been employed?

CHAPTER XIX.

THE subject of Junior finances is one that should be well considered. While the average Junior society does not need a great amount of money, yet it does need some; and this amount ought to be raised in a way that will be approved of by every Christian, and it ought to be considered as legitimate and as necessary as any work connected with the society.

Need of Money.—The society must have a small amount of money for its own expenses, varying with the size of the society. There is some printing that ought to be done, and probably every society could wisely make more use than it does of printer's ink, if it had the money. The printed prayer-meeting topics published by the United Society of Christian Endeavor are used by most Junior societies; and, though these do not cost much, yet they cost something and should be provided. There should also be some money that could be used in providing for a sociable at least once a year, though it is by no means necessary that there should be something to eat at every Junior social. Sometimes, too, the Juniors need new hymn-books, or something else that will help them in their work; and such things should be provided. The society ought also to give away some money every year, but that of course is a different matter, for the children themselves should in some way provide the money they wish to give away. If it is *called* their gift, it should be in reality their gift.

Ways of Providing for Society Expenses.—There are different ways of raising the money for the society expenses. Perhaps the best way is for the church to pay the bills just as it pays the Sunday-school bills. If in the judgment of the church the Junior society is doing a good work for the children, it ought to be supported; and, if it is not doing good work, then the church through the pastor or the older society should find out what is the trouble, and help to make things better. In some churches it is the custom for the older society to pay the expenses of the Junior society, and there are churches where the Junior superintendents pay these expenses out of their own pockets. Perhaps the children could earn enough money to pay their own expenses; but, since it is of necessity very little that they can earn or give, it seems better that they should give their money in benevolence, looking to the church for their own support just as in the home they look to their parents for support. In any case, the expenses of the average society are so small that there ought not to be any difficulty in providing for them.

How to Earn Missionary Money.—But the missionary money that they are to give away is another matter. Let that be their own gift, and help them to give generously and wisely, and with some self-sacrifice in time and money. Various plans for raising this money have been tried in different societies, such as giving out five-cent pieces for the children to invest in trading, and holding little sales and other schemes of this sort, many of which are more or less open to objection; but each society must decide for itself what is the best and most Christian way for the children to earn their missionary money. It would be a good plan at the beginning of each year to make the question of giving the subject of one meeting, and talk it all over prayerfully and carefully with the children, and help them up to the highest standard of Christian giving. Here are four plans that are suggested as possible and feasible, and good for most societies.

Giving the Tithe.—1. Ask each child who is willing to do so to pledge one-tenth of his income to the Lord. Explain that for them " income " means any money that " comes in " to them to do what they please with. Money that is given to them for a definite object must of course be used for that object; but money that is their own to use as they please can be tithed, and there ought to be a good many among the Juniors who would be willing to pledge themselves to do that. If they are unwilling, ask them to pledge it for one month or for three months on trial, and then perhaps they will be willing to continue it.

If any children are unwilling to take this pledge even for one month, perhaps they will be willing to promise to give to the Lord at least one cent a week out of their very own money. Try in some way to persuade them to begin by giving their own money to the Lord, cheerfully and heartily, because they love him.

Giving Time to the Lord.—2. After the children have given all they can of their own money, the total amount will probably be much smaller than what they would like to give away; so this second plan may be suggested to them. Ask each one who is willing to promise at least a half-hour of his time to the Lord every week. He may give the whole half-hour on Saturday, or five minutes each week-day, as seems best; and let him try in that time to earn some money for missions.

Many parents would be willing to pay their children at the rate of ten or twelve cents an hour for certain definite work regularly and faithfully done. Many parents are already doing that, that their children may earn some money for their own pleasure. Ask the children to give this one half-hour every week just to earn money for the Lord, not keeping any part of the amount for themselves. Just that one half-hour is the Lord's, and they can work other half-hours for themselves if they can find opportunity. It may not be possible for all your Juniors to try this plan, but probably some of them can. Some Juniors are already earning money by distributing papers, or running errands, or some other work. Ask *them* to accept this plan also; and, even if only a few of your Juniors do it, you will have added something to the missionary treasury, and the Juniors will have learned something more of the pleasure of service for Christ.

Mite-Boxes.—3. Let each child have a mite-box in which to keep his missionary earnings. You can get the boxes from your own missionary board, or your sunshine or whatsoever committee can make them. Let each child keep his mite-box in a conspicuous place at home, and talk about it till every

member of the household knows what it is for, and
occasionally pass it to his parents, or to some older
friends, that they may have an opportunity to contribute. Some parents and older brothers and sisters
might be glad to celebrate birthdays by putting in as
many pennies as they are years old. Of course the
children must be told that they are not to be too
urgent in their pleas for these gifts from their elders,
but it can do no harm to give these an occasional opportunity to make such a gift, especially as in many
families these same elders are giving nothing to missions. It may be objected to this plan that the children ought to give their money themselves, and not
ask it of the parents; but remember that they are not
to pass around their mite-boxes till they have first
given what they can themselves. This is not the first
plan suggested, but the third.

Entertainments.—4. If, having tried these three
plans, the children's offering is still smaller than it
ought to be, it may be thought best in some societies
to have an entertainment and raise some money in
that way. If you do this, try to make it also a lesson
in giving. Teach the children that they can please
Jesus by trying for his sake to earn money in this
way, and by doing their share of the work heartily, as
unto the Lord. For it means real work, and it is possible to have this work so done that it will mean to
the children real missionary Christian service.

Have your entertainment suitable to the place where
it is held, and have nothing in it that any parent can
object to. Plan it so that the children may give as little thought as possible to themselves or their dress, but

rather to the story they are telling or the pleasure they are giving. Charge a small admission, and make all those who come feel that they are getting their money's worth of pleasure.

There are many missionary entertainments that might be so planned that, while being exceedingly interesting to those who attend, they will also teach a missionary lesson to the children who take part. A literary or musical entertainment may be so planned as to be a real education to the children, and yet be very bright and amusing. Of course, a good entertainment means a certain amount of time for rehearsals, and sometimes these rehearsals must come at a time when the children would rather play; but, if for Christ's sake they are willing to give up some of their playtime to these rehearsals, that they may help the children who never heard of Him, it is real Christian service.

If this thought of doing it all for Christ's sake is kept before the children and before their superintendent, in planning and arranging for such an entertainment, there will be little danger of putting anything objectionable into it.

Reasons for an Entertainment Rather than a Sale. —I have suggested in this fourth plan an entertainment rather than a sale because it seems more probable that the children can give to those who patronize them the honest value of their money by an entertainment than that they could do so by a sale.

There are few things that children can make that their elders really want to buy, and there is much danger of putting too large a price on their work, or of too much urging to buyers ; and even those who are glad to do it for the sake of helping the children often buy things that they care nothing for, and do not know what to do with ; whereas almost any kind of an entertainment in which the children take part is sure to be of interest to their elders ; and, if the price of admission is not more than fifteen or twenty-five cents, it is highly probable that those who go will get the full value of their money. Even those who buy tickets simply to please the children, and do not care to go themselves, can usually find some one to whom to give the ticket who does care to go, and is pleased and grateful. In this case as in all others, however, the children should be cautioned not to urge their wares upon unwilling buyers. Let them simply offer their tickets ; and, if people do not wish to buy, let them accept the decision promptly and cheerfully.

A combination of these four plans, wisely and prayerfully carried out, ought to bring more than the usual amount of missionary money into almost any Junior treasury.

Right Methods of Raising Money.—In general, any method of raising money is right if it commends itself to an educated, sensitive conscience, and if your church and your pastor see no objection. Certainly the children should not use questionable methods. If you are in grave doubt about your plans, give them up, and try something else. Teach the children to be businesslike in their business, and fair and just in all their money matters.

Help them to have a real principle in everything connected with the raising of money and the spending of it, and help them to see that money in itself is nothing, and that the *love* of it is the " root of all evil." It is valuable only for what it will do; and, since most of us have not a large amount of it, we must use wisely what we have, and must not try to get it from others, except for a fair and honest equivalent.

Questions for Review.

(*a*)   How shall the Junior money be raised?
(*b*)   What use has the society for raising money?
(*c*)   Who shall pay the society expenses?
(*d*)   How shall the missionary money be raised?
(*e*)   What are some right and wrong methods of raising money?
(*f*)   Should money be raised by entertainments?

CHAPTER XX.

How Often to Hold Sociables.—The Junior sociables may be made a very helpful feature of the Junior Endeavor work if rightly managed. Just how often these Junior sociables shall be held must be decided by those who have them in charge ; but in general it may be said that they should be held just as often as is advantageous for your society, always remembering that they are of secondary importance in your work, and are of value only as they are a real help in your work for the children.

Some societies hold a sociable every month, and others hold only one or two in the course of a year. It should depend partly upon these questions : How many other social occasions do your children have to take up their time and their minds? As you conduct them, do you find them a real help in your Junior work?

Unless your children are mostly from the older boys and girls, these sociables ought usually to be held in the afternoon, at least in the winter months. In some societies they take the place immediately after the regular weekly meeting, making that meeting a little shorter if need be. Of course this plan can be followed only by those societies that hold their meeting on a week-day, but almost any society could plan for a

147

Saturday afternoon sociable, and could make it a very happy time for the children. Where the society is composed almost wholly of older boys and girls, it might perhaps be held at an early hour in the evening ; but as a rule there are more things to take the children out in the evening than their parents approve of, and the Junior superintendent ought not to add another unless she knows that the parents are willing.

Junior Social Committee.—These sociables for the children should always be under the charge of some older person. In a general way this like all the other Junior work should be under the supervision of the superintendent, but she may well leave the details in the hands of her helpers. The Junior social committee should feel the responsibility of planning the entertainment with the young lady from the Junior committee who has been appointed to help them. This older helper should feel herself responsible for the games chosen and for keeping a reasonable amount of order during the sociable, allowing no game or amusement that is likely to lead to too much boisterousness or confusion for the place where these gatherings must be held, and providing as much variety as possible. She should also feel a care for all the work of the social committee, such as making new members feel acquainted and at home, and helping children who may have recently come into town, or into the church or Sunday-school, to feel that they are among friends. Try in every way to cultivate a spirit of real friendliness among the members of this committee.

Sociables: How Carried on.—The sociables may consist of games, or musical or literary entertainment, or shadow pictures, or any kind of good time that children like and that is suitable for the gathering-place. Of course, if the meetings are held in the ladies' parlor of the church, or in the Sunday-school room, they will have to be planned a little differently from those held in a private parlor. The sociables should not be held too long, especially if for any reason they are held in the evening; and, while they should be really "good times," as children understand those words, yet the one who conducts them should be very strict in ruling out everything that the parents or the pastor would think improper or unsuitable.

There are plenty of games and amusements that are perfectly suitable and pleasant and amusing. Some societies make their sociables consist largely of recitations and readings and music, letting the children give selections that they have learned in school or with their music-teachers. Others provide suitable games, or shadow pictures, with an occasional stereopticon or graphophone entertainment, or something of that sort. You will find among the publications of the United Society of Christian Endeavor two or three little books that are full of suggestions for such gatherings.[1]

Who May Attend Sociables.—Different societies differ in their opinion as to who should be invited to these sociables, some opening their doors very wide that any children who wish may enter, and others limiting the attendance strictly to their own members. Of course it is understood in the beginning that only those children should come to whom these gatherings

[1] "Social Evenings," "Social to Save," and "Eighty Pleasant Evenings"; thirty-five cents each.

will be helpful in some way, and also that no children should attend them without an invitation.

These social gatherings should be considered as tools to help in our work, and unless they do that it is useless to hold them. Consider this question of invitations in the light of that thought, and you will be likely to make them include the right children. They ought, however, to be considered as a special treat; and the children will be more likely to think of them in that way if they can come only by invitation, rather than if any child who wishes may attend, whether he ever attends the meetings or not.

It is not necessary to send written invitations every time, though in small societies it might perhaps be well to do so, but ordinarily the invitations can be given to the children all at once at one of their regular meetings. The invitation ought usually to include all the active and preparatory members, and some who are not members at all; but as a rule do not invite to these gatherings children who have never attended the meetings and are not likely to do so.

Require of the children who come that they shall have attended some of the prayer-meetings, and that at least they have the intention to attend regularly. Notice any strangers who come to the sociables, and learn their names; ask whether this means that hereafter they expect to attend the prayer-meetings. If so, you are very glad to see them; or, if they are strangers in town and have come with some little friend, they are welcome; but let them distinctly understand that the sociables are not for those children who want only sociables and no prayer-meetings.

At the same time, it should be borne in mind that these sociables may perhaps be used to draw children into the meetings who otherwise would never think of coming. On this account take pains sometimes to send special invitations, perhaps written ones, to any children of whom you know, who ought to come to the meetings ; and tell them in your invitations that you hope they will have so good a time that they will want to come to the meetings afterwards.

Value of Sociables.—If the sociables are wisely planned, two or three objects ought to be accomplished by holding them. They ought to mean such happy good times to the children that even those who care nothing for the meetings will think it worth while to belong, if only for the sake of coming to the sociables. The preparatory membership has room for even such children as these ; and, if they will make the two promises required for that membership, then you have a hold on them and an opportunity to help them acquire an appetite for better things.

These sociables, too, afford opportunities for getting acquainted with the children in a way that would be impossible to one seeing them only at the meetings, and by entering heartily into their happy good times in this way a superintendent may sometimes get nearer to the hearts of some of the children than she ever could in any other way. For this reason all the superintendents should try to be at the sociables every time if it is possible. These sociables also help the children to get better acquainted with one another. There are, of course, a few children who seem to know almost everybody, and there are others who have their own special intimate friends; but at these sociables, at least, they all ought to be intimate friends, all trying to make every one else have a good time. Incidentally, too, these sociables may be made occasions when the children will unconsciously learn lessons in Christian courtesy and in gentleness and unselfishness and fairness in play. Teach these lessons quietly, without saying much about it, through these sociables, to all your Juniors, beginning with the social committee.

Education by Sociables.—But it may be said that, if these sociables are to be made occasions for inculcating moral lessons, there is danger that they will soon become so dull that the children will not care to attend them; but this by no means follows. It is quite possible to make these sociables educative in many ways, and at the same time very interesting and amusing, if they are planned with those purposes in mind. Of course the lessons in unselfishness, etc., will not be spoken lessons very often, but the children will unconsciously learn many of these lessons if the sociables are rightly conducted.

But a sociable may be made instructive as well as amusing. For instance, at one sociable try an old-fashioned spelling-match for fifteen minutes or half an hour, letting the Juniors choose sides and letting that side be considered victorious which is the largest at the end of the half-hour. Perhaps it might be well to get for such a sociable a list of some words that have been misspelled in school within a few days. Any day-school teacher would furnish you with such a list. Don't tell the children, however, that you are doing this. Learn the art of teaching your lessons without letting the children know that you meant to teach them. At another sociable one of the games might be a geographical game for which sides are chosen and judges appointed.

At another sociable give out missionary names to one set of children and to another set the names of the stations where the missionaries live, and let each one find her mate. But you will find in the books and booklets published by the United Society of Christian Endeavor especially for the social committee plenty of suggestions for all kinds of games, amusing and instructive and entertaining.

Real Object of All the Sociables.—Incidentally these sociables will help the Christian lives of the children, if the effort is made to have them teach such lessons as have been suggested. If one requisite for every game is that it shall be played fairly, the children will learn lessons in honesty. Sometimes, too, a story can be read which teaches a helpful lesson and is at the same time very bright and interesting. Sometimes stop in the middle of such a story, and let the children guess how it comes out, and tell how they would make it come out. Sometimes read half of a bright story, and appoint four or five of the older children to write a conclusion to it in five minutes, and give a prize to the one that the children vote to be the best.

But many of these moral lessons are and of necessity must be mainly incidental. Make the real object of your sociables to win the hearts of as many children as possible, that, having so won them, you may be able to win them for Christ.

Questions for Review.

(*a*) How often shall sociables be held ?
(*b*) Who shall have charge of them ?
(*c*) How shall they be conducted ?
(*d*) What kind of games may be allowed ?
(*e*) Who should be invited to these sociables ?
(*f*) What is the object of all the sociables ?
(*g*) Can these sociables be made both amusing and in-
         structive ?
(*h*) Can they in any way help the religious work of the
         society ?

CHAPTER XXI.

Age at Graduation.—The question of the age of the Juniors is a variable one according to conditions and circumstances, but the members should usually be included within the ages of five and fifteen. Some societies graduate their Juniors at fourteen and some at fifteen or even sixteen; but, if there are many little children in the society,—and there ought to be in most societies,—it would seem that the limit ought not to be above fifteen, and in many cases fourteen would be better.

It is not necessary, however, to draw a hard and fast line which can never under any circumstances be crossed. Make your regular limit fourteen or fifteen as you think best, but in special circumstances for special reasons make exceptions if it seems best. Some children are brighter than others, and some are more earnest than others; and in uncertain cases do what in your best judgment seems best for the particular child and for the whole society. As a rule, however, every child ought to stay in the Junior society at least till he is old enough to enter the high school, which some societies make the dividing line; and most children ought to go then, even if they might like to stay a little longer in the Junior society.

If a member who is over fifteen expresses a

preference for the Junior society, have a quiet little talk with him and find his reasons; and, if they seem to you good ones, and you believe that on the whole it would be better for him to remain a Junior a little longer, let him do so. It is better, however, to have a definite rule and adhere to it as closely as circumstances will permit, and, when you make exceptions, have a special vote to suspend the rule for that occasion for reasons that seem to you wise and good.

Ask the older society to help you in keeping the Juniors in their own society as long as may seem best by voting not to receive any children until they have reached a certain age, unless by special request of the Junior superintendent. Then the children themselves will have a clear understanding that unless there is some special reason for making a change they are expected to enter the Junior society as little children and to stay there until they are fourteen or fifteen, and then to graduate at once into the older society. Try so to plan for them, and talk things over with them as a matter of course, that it will never occur to them that they could drop out wholly, as some children have done when they began to feel themselves too old for the Junior society.

Preparation for Graduation.—The children ought not, however, to enter the older society without a little special preparation. It is a good plan to have regular times for graduation twice a year, so that several children shall graduate together, and shall expect to go into the older society at a special time. It is much easier, too, for the children themselves to go in little companies of two or three or more, than for each one to graduate separately when he reaches the required age.

Christian Endeavor Day is a good time to take this advance step, and is about in the middle of the church year, and the last Sunday in June is better than the first in September or October, because there is a little danger that in their summer absence from home and from the society some of the children might find their good resolutions oozing out, and might incline to drop out entirely. It is better to advance them in June before they scatter for the vacation, and then when they come back they are already members of the older society, and are all ready to take their place in its work. If you choose these dates, begin just after the Week of Prayer to prepare your graduation class. Invite all those children who have become fourteen since last June to stop for a little after-meeting when the other children go home. At this little meeting, where you will have perhaps only two or three or half a dozen, the children will talk frankly and freely.

Take time to talk over thoroughly the pledge as used in the older society, and the respects in which it differs from the Junior pledge. Show them that going into the older society means promotion to larger and higher service; it means promising something more, and it means doing more and better committee work. Find out what part of the pledge they find it hardest to promise, and strengthen them in the places where they most need it. If they dread taking part in the meeting of the older ones, suggest that they take part in the very first part of the meeting.

Urge that they begin in the very first meeting to

express at least one thought on the topic, and not be content with saying just a Bible verse. If they are troubled about the " regular Sunday and mid-week services," talk that over with them, and show them that if they are Christians they ought to attend these meetings, whether they promise it or not. While they were little children, perhaps they could not go regularly to evening meetings ; but they are older now, and they can be promoted to that larger service. Help them to think of it all as an honor and a privilege to serve God in this larger way.

Perhaps you can help them by also speaking a word to their Sunday-school teachers and by suggesting that, whenever they can do so, they take two or three minutes of their time in Sunday-school in talking over the Endeavor topic, and so help their scholars to have a thought on the topic that they can express. If necessary, have two or three of these little after-meetings with this graduating class. Take it for granted that they are all going to graduate into the older society, unless there is some special reason why they should remain Juniors for a little time ; but do not suggest the possibility of their dropping out. There is much less danger that they will want to drop out when several graduate together than there would be if each one should graduate when he reaches the proper age, and the graduation can also wisely be made a special occasion in the older society when these new recruits are taken into the ranks.

Graduation Exercises. — Different societies have their own graduation exercises for the boys and girls who leave them, and many different methods of wel-

coming them into the older society have been tried.
The simplest are probably the best, but it is wise to
mark the occasion in some way.   At the last Junior
meeting when these children attend have some special exercises.   Perhaps have a special graduation song
that may be sung while the graduates stand, and then
let the superintendent or some of her helpers offer a
prayer for these boys and girls who are going to be
promoted to larger and higher service, that they may
be found faithful, and may be helpful and useful and
consistent members of the older society to which
they go.

If there are any preparatory members to graduate,
have another prayer for them that in the older society
they may be led to give themselves to Christ, and to
place themselves on the side with those who love his
service.   But, if faithful work has been done in the
Junior society, there ought not to be many preparatory members to graduate.   The hearts of little children are easily reached, and it ought to be possible to
lead them to Christ before they are old enough to
graduate.   Strive and pray to do this in your society.

In some special way these graduate Juniors should
also be welcomed into the older society, with some
song of welcome, or words of welcome by the pastor,
and perhaps with some little token of welcome.   Perhaps the best thing to give to these new Christian Endeavorers is the little booklet by Prof. Amos R.
Wells, called " The Endeavor Greeting," which wel-
comes them to membership and very helpfully sug-
gests ways of working.   Some societies give also
a Christian Endeavor pin to every Junior graduate

when he enters the society, with the suggestion that
he wear it always and remember what it means.
Sometimes the pastor might speak the words of welcome, and sometimes the president of the society,
or the chairman of the lookout committee. The
method matters not: the chief thing is the welcome.
Make that unmistakable.

Work for the Graduates.—When these Juniors
have once entered the older society, set them to work
at once. The very best plan that I have seen tried or
heard recommended is this: Have in the society a
Whatsoever and a Lend-a-Hand committee; appoint
some of your wisest and most winning workers as
chairmen of these committees, having a young man
for chairman of the lend-a-hand committee, and a
young lady for chairman of the whatsoever committee.
As soon as the Juniors have been received into
the society, place the boys on the lend-a-hand and
the girls on the whatsoever committee. Let the
leaders of these committees hold frequent committee
meetings, and try in every way to help these boys
and girls to be faithful to the promises they have made.

Help them to think of something to say in the
prayer-meeting. Use your inventive faculty to think
of work for them to do. Both these committees
should find their own work, doing little things that
ought to be done and that no one else is doing, and
being ready always to help any other committee that
needs their services. Some such committees have
mended the church carpets, and glued on the backs
of the Bibles and hymn-books, and rubbed out pencil
marks, and covered the books for the Sunday-school

library, and looked up stray books and stray scholars for the Sunday-school; and many other such like things they do.

If the chairman of each of these committees can, for the first meeting at least, invite their committee to tea, and have a social evening with them, it will greatly help to mutual friendship, and make the rest of the work easier. The leaders of these committees should feel it their privilege to be a real help to these boys and girls in every possible way. The whatsoever and lend-a-hand committees may be made a real means of grace to their members, and may start these boys and girls in the path of efficient Christian service.

Questions for Review.

(*a*)   At what age should Juniors graduate?
(*b*)   How shall they be prepared for graduation?
(*c*)   How should it be made sure that they do not drop out between the two societies?
(*d*)   Should they graduate singly or in groups?
(*e*)   When is a good time for graduation-day?
(*f*)   How should the Juniors be welcomed into the older society?
(*g*)   How can they be cared for there and introduced to the work?

CHAPTER XXII.

The Duty of the Christian Endeavor Society to the Juniors.—The relation between the Young People's Christian Endeavor society and the Junior society should be a very close one. The members of the older society should be kept informed concerning the work of the children, by monthly reports from either the superintendent or one of her helpers, and should be ready at any time to extend a helping hand to the children. Sometimes, perhaps as often as once a year, the older society might give a sociable especially for the Juniors, when the members should exert themselves to make a very pleasant time for the Juniors, serving light refreshments if possible, and planning some bright and entertaining and helpful exercises to interest the children.

Sometimes the older executive committee might invite the Junior officers to meet with them in their deliberations, and thus give the Juniors a helpful lesson in transacting the business of the society. One such meeting ought to help the Juniors to do very much better work in planning the work of their own society.

Sometimes, too, there should be a union prayer-meeting led by the presidents of the two societies, which should be very carefully planned that it may be made as helpful as possible. Occasionally the president or some of the other members of the older society should be ready to go and speak a few words in the Junior meeting. As often as possible some young man from the older society might speak at the Junior temperance meetings,.that the boys may hear a talk on temperance from a young man's standpoint.

The Junior Committee.—There should also be in every older society a Junior committee, who should stand ready to help the Junior superintendent in every possible way, wherever she needs their help. All these things, and many others, as opportunity opens, the Juniors have a right to expect from their older brothers and sisters.

What the Juniors Can Do for the Christian Endeavor Society.—And now what may the older Endeavorers expect from the Juniors? Very much the same help that the older brothers and sisters in a family expect from the younger ones. A good many little favors and kindnesses the younger ones can do for their elders, and they ought to be glad to do them.

Sometimes the flower committee of the older society will be very glad of help that the Juniors can give in collecting flowers for decorations for special occasions. Sometimes the music committee would like a little help from the Junior choir for some special meeting. Sometimes the Junior sunshines can help the older whatsoevers in their work. Sometimes the Junior minutemen can help by running errands, and in many little ways like these the boys and girls can show themselves to be very useful members of the church family. If in such ways as these the two socicties show themselves mutually helpful, their relationship will always be a very close one, and they will always rejoice to be workers *together* for Christ and his church.

Responsibility of Christian Endeavorers for the Juniors.—In some churches it has happened that the older society has gone on its way, knowing little or nothing about the Junior work, and apparently caring less. This is probably due partly to thoughtlessness on their part, and partly to the fact that they have not been kept in touch with the Junior society by frequent reports of their work. These reports ought regularly to be called for when the committees give their reports at the monthly business meeting, and this will help the older young people to see that they, too, have some responsibility for the Junior work.

Sometimes the pastor might be asked to preach a sermon on the work of young people in the church, and their responsibility for the children. Sometimes let the Junior secretary read the monthly report at the business meeting of the older society. In this way, by keeping the older society always informed concerning the work of the Juniors, by inviting them occasionally to the Junior meetings, and by occasionally asking their help, the members of the Young People's Christian Endeavor society may be led to feel their own responsibility for sharing, to some extent at least, in the work for the children of the church.

Union Meetings.—Whenever it is thought best to have a union meeting of the two societies, plan a careful programme for such a meeting, letting the two presidents lead it, and taking pains to make sure that every active member of each society shall take part briefly in the meeting.   In some societies it may seem advisable to hold such a meeting as often as twice a year, and sometimes one of these meetings might be appointed for the time when the graduate Juniors are to be received into the older society, making it a farewell and a welcome at the same time.

When a union sociable is held, every senior should take pains to speak to every Junior, and it may be made such a merry, friendly time that it will be a real help to the boys and girls who shall attend, as well as to the older young people.   Suggestions for such an evening may be found in the publications devoted to the work of the social committee.

Working Together.—So far we have talked of the separate work of the two societies, and of their relation to each other and occasional fellowship; but both societies have a work to do for the church, and some of this work they may do *together.*   Together they may decorate the church for Christmas or Easter or any other special occasion.   Together they may make their presence and their help felt in the Sunday-school, showing by their regular and faithful attendance, and by their conscientious study of the Bible, that this Sunday-school hour is a real privilege given to them by the church.

Sometimes the two societies can together take charge of one of the regular missionary meetings of the church if desired.   Sometimes they can let their voices be heard in the church prayer-meetings if desired, the younger ones perhaps by repeating a Bible verse, and the older ones by expressing a thought of their own on the topic ; and all together they can help to make the singing what it should be in the church prayer-meeting.

Together they can help to support their own church, by contributing something, even though it must be only a little, to the expenses of the church, and by faithful attendance on Sunday mornings, and, in the case of those who are old enough, on Sunday evenings.

In every possible way the Christian Endeavorers and Junior Endeavorers should help each other to feel that the church is for them and they for the church, and that it is their duty and privilege to work together, and to help in every way possible to make their own church a power in the community.

Questions for Review.

(*a*) What can the Juniors expect from the seniors?

(*b*) What can the seniors expect from the Juniors?

(*c*) How can the older Endeavorers be made to feel their responsibility for the Juniors?

(*d*) How may union meetings and sociables be made helpful ?

(*e*) What can the two societies do *together* for the church ?

CHAPTER XXIII.

CHURCH-MEMBERSHIP FOR THE JUNIORS.

Deciding for Christ.—If a Junior society is what it should be, it ought to be expected to lead the children into the Christian life and into church-membership. It should be a part of the work of the Junior superintendent to prepare the children for this step, but this work should be very carefully done. So serious a step as that to church-membership should not be lightly taken.

The first thing should be to bring the children to decide for Christ and to begin the Christian life, and for this purpose special evangelistic meetings should be held, though there ought to be something in every Junior Endeavor prayer-meeting that would make the children want to lead a Christian life, and would strengthen them in doing it. Still, it is not so easy to get at a child's heart, and find out why he is not a Christian, and show him how to be one, in a large meeting, with all kinds of children present.

Decision Day.—Sometimes the children may be helped by having the Christian life carefully explained to them in a general meeting, and then by an earnest appeal to them to begin now to serve the Lord. Then after this meeting appoint a short after-meeting for all the boys and girls who want to be Christians, or who do not quite know whether they are Christians or not ;

and in this smaller meeting, where only two or three, or perhaps half a dozen, will be found, talk more directly and plainly to them as individuals, asking them lovingly and simply just what it is that they do not understand, and telling them just how they can begin the Christian life.

Some societies have " Decision Day" on the first meeting in February, Christian Endeavor Day,—and try to bring the decision then. It seems a beautiful and appropriate celebration of Christian Endeavor Day to strive each year to win some Juniors to Christ. Others hold such meetings on New Year's Day, or at the beginning of the church year, or whenever there seems to be any special interest among the children.

Special Evangelistic Meetings.—Such special meetings should be held as frequently as it seems wise, and the superintendent should study to understand and explain very simply just what the Christian life means and how to begin it. Sometimes it may be wise to ask the pastor or some older church-member to come to one of these special meetings to talk with the children. Whatever methods may be used, the one object should be to help the boys and girls to become Christians, and the whole work of the society should be made helpful to their Christian lives.

Preparation for Church-Membership.—When the superintendent has reason to believe that any of her Juniors are living truly Christian lives, and when they seem ready, so far as she can judge, for church-membership, the next step should be to talk with their parents before saying anything about church-membership directly to the children themselves. In a general way the thought should always be kept before the children that one who is really a Christian ought to be willing to make it known, and ought to expect sometime to become a member of the church ; but just when that time shall be must be decided in each case separately, and ought never to be decided without consultation with the parents of the child.

Go and talk with the father or mother or both, and tell them plainly that their child seems to you to be a Christian, and ought in your judgment to consider the question of uniting with the church, but that it seemed right to talk first with the parents.

If they themselves are Christian people, they will be glad to hear this, even if they do not think it wise just yet for their child to unite with the church. It is quite likely that they will feel a more watchful and sympathetic care of this young Christian, and will begin to consider the question of church-membership if they have not already done so. If they are not Christians, it is possible that this talk about the welfare of their child may lead them to consider the question of their own lives ; and it may sometimes happen that a father and a mother may be led into the Kingdom by their own child. After consulting the parents, if they do not object, have an earnest talk with the children who seem ready for church-membership, and explain to them simply what church-membership means, and why it is the duty of a Christian ; and let them talk, and explain their own views on the subject, and ask any questions they wish. Having talked it all over with them, kneel down with the children, and ask all who are willing, to pray about it, and to ask God to show them just what he wants them to do, and to make them willing to do his will, whatever it may be.

Do not *urge* the children. If they do wish to unite with the church, it should be their own decision, and they should be made to understand clearly that they ought not to do it simply because they think their parents or their superintendents wish it, but only because they believe God wishes them to do it. If they do not feel sure of that, help them, if they wish, to know how they may understand God's will for them; and, when they do enter the church, let it be by their own intelligent wish and choice. Make the way into the church easy for them, and open the door wide, but do not push them through it. Let them go in voluntarily and earnestly and sincerely.

At What Age Children May Become Church-Members.—The question of how early a child may enter the church is one that is often discussed, but the wisest and most earnest Christians have come to believe that it is not a question of age. Some children of ten years may enter more fully prepared for the step than others of fourteen or fifteen. It is a question of *heart* preparation; help the children to " prepare their hearts to seek the Lord," and, if their lives show that they love him, let that be the test.

One of the most earnest and consistent and most active Christians in the church to which I belong united with that church when he was eight years old, and no one has ever doubted that he was at that age fitted to take his place in the church; but that would not be the case with every child, of course. Let the superintendent decide, so far as her own responsibility goes, for each child by himself; and, when she has talked with the parents and the children, and believes them to be ready, let her hand their names to the pastor, telling him her reasons for believing them ready for church-membership. If he thinks best, the superintendent might herself go with the children to talk with their pastor, unless the parents prefer to take them.

Preparing the Children Individually.—We have spoken of what the superintendent may do for the children in presenting this matter to them; but it should not be forgotten that the final decision should rest with the child himself, and his parents, and his pastor. Do not attempt to decide this question for any child, and be careful not to *urge* them. This question of church-membership should usually be considered outside of the regular meetings of the society. Talk with the children individually as they seem ready for it, but do not ask any of them to decide such a question in the general meeting. Children have usually too much of a " follow-my-leader " sort of spirit, and there is danger that one child may wish to take this step because another is going to take it; and, if the question were asked in the general meeting how many thought they were ready for church-membership, it is quite likely that several children would raise their hands who had really given very little thought to the matter. Let it be an individual matter, then, presented to the children one at a time, as they seem ready for it.

The Children and the Church Covenant.—If in the judgment of the child and his parents he is ready to present himself to the church committee, then there should be some special preparation for church-membership besides what his parents may give him. In some churches the pastor will wisely think that this work is his to do, and he will form a church-preparation class for a few of the boys and girls.

If for any reason he does not do this, then the Junior superintendent should do it. Have some little special meetings with these children for three or four weeks before the Sunday on which they are to unite with the church, and go over the church covenant with them, and perhaps the simplest form of the creed. Help them to understand that when a person becomes a member of a church he makes some definite promises to that church and to God. Go over the covenant with them very carefully, that they may understand just what these promises are. Let them rewrite the creed in their own language, simply writing out in their own words just what they understand that they are to covenant and promise to God and his church. Hold at least three or four of these little special church preparation meetings, till all that is possible has been done to prepare them to enter the church with a full understanding of the obligations they are taking upon themselves.

The Children in the Church.—When the children have once become church-members, it too often happens that the church seems to take it for granted that everything needful has been done, and now the children are all right, whereas now is just the time when they need careful guarding and shepherding. Unless some one else is doing this work, the Junior superintendent should feel a care to help the children to faithfulness to their vows, not only through her words in the usual Christian Endeavor prayer-meetings, but in a little special preparatory service held before each communion service for those Juniors who are church-members. These special meetings might well be held on the week of the usual preparatory lecture in the church, and it should be made to mean to the children what this service means to the older members of the church, a preparation for coming to the Lord's table.

At such little preparatory meetings read with the children the story of the Lord's Supper ; let them explain to you what they think it means, and why it is celebrated so often in the churches. Call it sometimes " The Memory Supper," and ask them what it is to help them remember. Ask them whether they pray when they bow their heads after taking the bread and the wine, and help them to know how to pray and commune with Christ at that time. Try to make this communion service mean to them what it does to the older members of the church. Try through these little meetings and in every possible way to guard and guide these children, who have come into the church and confessed Christ before men.

Special Meetings, Why ?—It may seem that in these chapters I am recommending very frequent special meetings of various kinds ; but such little quiet meetings with a very few children may be made so exceedingly helpful that it seems worth while that the superintendent should be willing to give time for this work. It is perhaps the most important work that can be done in connection with the Junior society. These little special meetings need not usually be very long, however; generally ten or fifteen minutes would be better than a longer time.

Which Shall Come First, Church-Membership or Admission to the Society?—I have said nothing here to indicate whether the boys and girls should be church-members before they become active members of the society. Some societies think very decidedly that church-membership should come first. Others think that church-membership is a more solemn and important step, and that the taking of the active member's pledge in the Junior society may be for many children the first step in the beginning of their Christian life, and that this is the place to prepare for church-membership. Some parents, too, who hope and believe that their children are Christians, are yet unwilling that they should become church-members while so young, but would allow them to become active members of the Junior society, and in this way show to those who know them that they want to give themselves to Christ. Let your church and your pastor decide this question for you, but in some way try to lead the children into the Christian life, and do what can be done to fit them for church-membership.

Questions for Review.

(*a*) How would you help the children to decide for Christ?

(*b*) How early may a child unite with the church?

(*c*) Who shall decide when he is ready?

(*d*) What preparation for church-membership can the society give to the children?

(*e*) What can the society do for the children after they are in the church ?

(*f*) How would you help the children to understand the meaning of the Lord's Supper ?

CHAPTER XXIV.

Working Together for the Children.—In many ways it is possible for the Sunday-schools and day-schools and the Junior Endeavor society to help one another. Through all three of these agencies we are trying to help our boys and girls to the best possible development of all their powers, and it is a matter of course that these agencies will all accomplish more if they work together, supplementing and aiding one another.

Too often at present these different agencies for the education and training of the young work independently, and, while perhaps not hindering one another, yet fail of some results that they might accomplish if there could be occasional consultations by the day-school teacher and the Sunday-school teacher and the Junior superintendent, each of whom views the child from a different angle, and sees a different side of his character.

The Junior Endeavor Society Helping the Sunday-School.—There are some ways in which the Junior Endeavor society ought to help the work of the Sunday-school. For instance, there might be in the Junior society a Sunday-school committee, whose

176

work should be to do everything possible to help the Sunday-school. Such a committee might be always on the lookout for new scholars whom they might invite to the Sunday-school. Through the other members of the society they might find out when new boys and girls move into their town or into their streets, and might invite these to go with them to Sunday-school, perhaps calling for them the first two or three Sundays. Through their day-school, too, they ought to be able to find boys and girls who do not attend any Sunday-school, but would perhaps do so if invited.

Looking up Absent Members of the Sunday-School. —This committee might also look up absent and missing members of the Sunday-school. Through the Sunday-school superintendent it might easily come to be understood that any teacher should hand to some member of this committee the name of any boy or girl in his class who is absent, and this Junior would see that some member of his committee should in the course of the week look up the missing scholar and find the reason of his absence, and let him know that his teacher missed him, and hoped for his return on the next Sabbath. If any of these absent members are ill, the Sunday-school committee might notify the sunshine committee, and in some way they might express their sympathy by sending flowers or a card or some little delicacy.

Looking up Missing Sunday-School Books.—This committee might also be asked to look up Sunday-school books that have been kept out more than the allotted time. The librarian could give to this committee the names and addresses of those to whom such books are charged and ask that they call for them.

Setting a Good Example in Sunday-School.—This committee should also be expected to do all it can to help to keep order in the Sunday-school. They can begin by setting a very good example themselves, and so far as their influence reaches they can exert it with other boys and girls. Perhaps it might be well that they should sometimes report in their Junior prayer-meeting certain classes who appear to them to have been setting good examples of quietness and reverent attention to their lessons.

If the Juniors know that it is a part of the regular work of their society to help keep good order in the Sunday-school, it will have some influence with many of them. These are a few things that a Junior Sunday-school committee might do to help the Sunday-school, and a wise and efficient superintendent will doubtless think of many more.

If any Junior society is so small that it can have only a few committees, some of this work might be done by the prayer-meeting or the lookout committee, or it might be considered the work of the whole society; but in some way every Junior society ought to be made to feel that their Christian endeavor extends as far as the Sunday-school.

The Sunday-School Helping the Junior Society. —If the Junior Endeavor society can help the Sunday-school, it is equally true that the Sunday-school can help the Junior society. The notice of the Junior prayer-meeting and the topic which is to be considered might be given every Sunday in the Sunday-school, and sometimes a word from the superintendent will quicken the interest of the Sunday-school scholars who never go to the Junior meetings, so that they will want to attend at least once or twice ; and, when they are once there, the Junior superintendent should make it her business so to interest and help them that they will want to come again.

If every Sunday-school teacher who has boys and girls in her class would take the first two or three minutes of lesson-time to talk over the Junior topic with her boys and girls, she would help them to know how to take part in Junior meeting, and to understand the topic. There are some boys and girls in our Junior societies who get very little help at home, and a few words from their Sunday-school teacher would be very helpful to them.

The Sunday-school teacher, too, can occasionally ask questions about the Junior meeting, and express her interest in it, and perhaps occasionally attend the Junior meeting, being prepared to say a few words there if desired, or at least to express to the Junior superintendent her willingness to help her in the work as she has opportunity. A Sunday-school teacher who has seen her scholars in their Junior Endeavor meeting will know them a little better, and be better able to help them through her own work in the Sunday-school.

The Junior Superintendent and the Day–School.— The same methods that have been suggested for combined work through the Junior society and the Sunday-school may be used also, with some variations, in the day-schools. A Junior superintendent who wants to do the best possible work for her boys and girls ought to go occasionally to the day-schools, that she may know her Juniors there, and may see how they are living the truths of which they speak and pray in the Junior meetings.

She might give to each teacher a list of the active members of the Junior Endeavor society who are in her class, and ask her to observe their efforts to be faithful to the pledge they have taken, and to suggest ways in which their superintendent may help them to be more faithful. Enlist the sympathy of the day-school teacher in your work, and you have another ally.

Let the Juniors know that you are interested in the work they are doing at day-school, and that being a Christian means being a Christian in school. Take an interest in their marks when they receive their quarterly reports, especially their marks in deportment, and commend those who have been faithful, bearing in mind that some of those who have lower marks may perhaps have worked harder than some of those who have higher marks. It is diligence and faithfulness that should be commended.

Geography in Junior Endeavor Societies.—The Junior society may also be of some help to the children in their studies. At least in geography their Junior work ought to count towards their school-work, and perhaps also a little in a literary way ; for the missionary meetings will incidentally give them many lessons in geography, and in their sociables there ought to be some readings and recitations that will help to give them a taste for good literature. Sometimes invite a day-school teacher to come to a missionary-meeting or a sociable or to one of the regular prayer-meetings of the society, that she may see what you are trying to do for her boys and girls, and how you are also trying to help her.

The School-Teacher and Junior Endeavor.—The day-school teacher may also do something if she will to help the work of the Junior society, by talking about it with her scholars, by visiting it occasionally and thus showing her sympathy with their Christian work, and occasionally by suggesting to the Junior superintendent topics that might well be spoken of in the meetings. If the Junior society meets on a week-day, the teacher might plan not to keep any of the Juniors after school on the evening of their meeting, telling them, if need be, that she has so planned it because she believes that their Junior meeting will help them to do better work in school next time.

Perhaps once or twice a year there might be some teacher who would be willing to go to the Junior meeting prepared to give to the boys and girls a fifteen-minute talk on their topic. It will surely help her own influence in the school if she meets the children from this common ground of service to Christ, and it will be good for the children occasionally to hear in their meeting from some one whose regular work with them is so different.

Try some of these methods, or some variation of them, in your society, and see whether you do not find them helpful.

Questions for Review.

(*a*) How can the Juniors help the Sunday-school ?

(*b*) How can the Sunday-school help the Junior society ?

(*c*) How can the Junior society help the day-schools ?

(*d*) Can the teachers be expected to do anything for the society ?

CHAPTER XXV.

The Parents and the Children.—We have already spoken of the way in which the children may be helped in their lives by various different agencies, but there is no one from whom the Junior superintendent ought so confidently to expect help as from the parents of the children; and, though sometimes complaints have been made that very little help comes from this source, yet I believe it might come, and would come, from properly directed efforts to obtain it.

I believe that all fathers and mothers, even those who do not seem to make any great efforts in that direction themselves, desire their children to be good. They want their children to rise higher in every way than they are themselves; and, if they understand exactly what the Junior superintendent is trying to do for their children, they are glad.

The Superintendent and the Parents.—But sometimes Christian parents seem to show very little interest in the work of the society, it is said. If this is the case, is it not possible that the Junior superintendent is also partly to blame for it? Keep yourself in touch with the parents; call on them occasionally; and let them know just what you are doing, and why, and how you want their help. I believe there are parents who would gladly lend their assistance if they knew

183

just what to do. *Tell* them definitely what you would like to have them do.

If the parents would ask their children every week about their Junior meeting, and what they talked and prayed about, and how they mean to profit by it, and what their superintendent said, it would show their interest; and, though the children might not at first carry home any very clear and definite reports of the work of their society, they would in time learn to do it. If the parents would also talk over the topic with the children before the meeting, and help them to prepare to take part in it, they would be more ready to enter into the children's Christian lives, and could better help them, besides perhaps gaining some help for their own lives. For there is no way to bring a thought so plainly home to one's own self as to try to make it clear to a child.

The Mothers at the Meetings.—While it is true that not all mothers are gifted as speakers, there must be some mothers of Juniors who could occasionally go to the Junior meeting, and give a very helpful talk to the boys and girls on their topic. Even those mothers who feel that they cannot help in this way can show their interest and sympathy by going at least once a year to a Junior meeting to listen to the words spoken and the prayers offered there.

Mothers' Meetings.—There should also be in every church some kind of a mothers' association, whose object should be to pray for the conversion of the children, and to help them in their Christian lives, and also to influence the lives of other mothers who are not Christians. In some churches there are already formed Mothers' Endeavor societies, working along Christian Endeavor lines, and co-operating so far as possible with the superintendent of the Junior society in her work.

What the Mothers' Meeting May do for the Juniors.—Such societies have a simple form of the Christian Endeavor pledge, binding their members to lead a Christian life and to take some part in their own prayer-meetings, and to do whatever they can to assist the Junior society. Other churches have Maternal Associations of various kinds, all having the same general object. Such a society may do much to help in the Junior work by enlisting all the mothers of Juniors and by consulting with the superintendent as to the ways in which they may manifest their sympathy and their desire to help. In this mothers' society the Junior secretary might occasionally read a report of the work of the Junior society. The mothers' meeting might also be furnished with a copy of the Junior topics, that they may know what the Juniors are praying for; and occasionally both societies might take the same topic, when it seems a suitable one, looking at it in one meeting from the standpoint of the mothers and in the other from that of the children.

Perhaps once a year the mothers might give the children a sociable, at which the mothers should also be present, the children providing some kind of literary or musical entertainment, and the mothers providing refreshments, having also a speaker who shall represent the mothers, though not necessarily chosen from their own number. Perhaps, also, it might be possible once a year to have a union meeting, in which each society should hold a half-hour meeting by itself, and then they should have a half-hour together. Some mothers' societies have also a custom of giving occasionally some little devotional book to each Junior, such as Miss Havergal's " Little Pillows," or " Morning Bells," or a " Daily Food." Such gifts are good for the children to receive, and they help also to show the interest and sympathy of all the mothers for all the children.

Parents' Endeavor Societies.—Some few churches have organized Parents' Endeavor societies, in which both the fathers and mothers pledge themselves to work for their children's conversion and growth in the Christian life. Perhaps it might be possible occasionally to find a father of a Junior who would give some thought to the Junior Endeavor society, and would help it in any way he can. A talk to the boys from the standpoint of the father would sometimes be the most helpful influence that could be brought to bear upon them.

Critical Mothers.—It is sometimes complained that the parents are unsympathetic and critical, and hinder rather than help the work of the Junior society. If this is ever the case, it is more likely to be through some misunderstanding of the work done than for any other reason. Sometimes, too, there may be real ground for criticism, which perhaps the Junior superintendent herself recognizes, though she finds herself unable to remedy the defects in her work, which she sees more plainly than any one else.

The Superintendent and the Mothers.—Why not go, then, to the parents whom you think to be un-

sympathetic, and tell them something of your difficulties, and ask for their sympathy and help? Do
not, if you can avoid it, go to any parent to complain
of her children, but rather tell her what you are trying
to do for all the children, and how much you feel your
own weakness, and how earnestly you desire to be a
real help to the children. Invite her to come in
once in a while to see what you are trying to do, and
to make suggestions for improvement in your work.

Be ready to receive criticisms and suggestions, and
make them a help; for they probably point out some
defects in the work itself. It may not be easy to take
them, but the Father can give you grace to receive
them graciously, and to profit by them. Perhaps the
meetings have not been as orderly and reverent as
they should be. Let some of the parents tell you how
they think you could make them more so.

In some way keep in touch with the mothers and
make them your friends, and they will be glad to help
and not hinder your work for their children. Once in
a while, too, have a mothers' meeting with your Juniors, sending a special invitation by each member of
the society to his own mother to come and make the
meeting one which will be a help to the mothers as
well as to the children. There are some topics given
every year that would be very good for such a meeting.

Consulting Together.—In some churches it would
certainly be possible to plan as often as once a year
for a social gathering of the mothers and fathers and
day-school and Sunday-school teachers with the Junior superintendents. Perhaps the pastor would help
plan such a gathering, and would himself be one of

the speakers.   Let the Junior superintendent at this gathering give a report of her work, and tell some of the encouraging and some of the discouraging things she has met with; and she might also take this opportunity to ask for any special help that she needs from parents or teachers or pastor.

Ask one of the fathers to speak a few words about the children, and how they need help; and perhaps have also a few words from at least one teacher from the day-school, and one from the Sunday-school, and let the pastor have the closing remarks.   Then, with light refreshments and an opportunity for social intercourse, all these people who are working in their separate ways for the same children may have opportunity for an interchange of opinions and for suggestions and kindly criticisms, which ought to result in better work all around for our boys and girls, who are growing up in the church and learning to find their place and their work there.

Questions for Review.

(*a*)   How can the parents help the Junior society?
(*b*)   What can a mothers' society do for the Juniors?
(*c*)   What can be done if parents are unsympathetic or critical?
(*d*)   What are the possibilities from consultation with parents?

CHAPTER XXVI.

Object of a Junior Union.—The object of a Junior union is in the main the same as that of a Junior society, to develop and strengthen the Christian lives of those who join it, and to help them in their work for the boys and girls. A Junior union ought also to work for the increasing of the number of societies in its own district and the strengthening of the work of those already existing.

There ought to be a Junior union in every district where there are several Junior societies within reach of each other. A model constitution for a Junior union will be found in the appendix to this book.

Membership in the Union.—Aside from the annual rally it is not expected that the children will regularly attend the meetings of the union, which are largely for the superintendent, assistant superintendent, and other older Junior workers. Every society in the district should be represented in the meetings of the union by its Junior superintendent and assistant superintendent, and, if possible, by at least one member of the Junior committee. It is through the interchange of methods and experiences that help will come to the superintendents. A method that has been tried in one society very successfully may not be exactly suited for another; but sometimes it will be found to be just the thing, and, if not, often some variation of it will make it right. But many of the problems of Junior Endeavor are the same in all societies, and one who has successfully met and conquered them can by telling her experience help others. Sometimes, too, a worker of long and tried experience may be found who will give at a meeting of the Junior union such a helpful talk as will be of great value to younger and more inexperienced workers.

It ought to be the case that in every Christian Endeavor society a future Junior superintendent is being trained for future work, and for this reason the assistant superintendent and at least one or two of the Junior committee ought to attend the meetings of the Junior union, that they may hear the work discussed, and may be preparing for the time when it may rest upon their shoulders.

Union Meetings.—The meetings of a Junior union should be held often enough to keep up interest in the work, and to discuss sufficiently often those questions that are always coming up in children's work. Some unions hold their meetings every month, and others once in two months. Some think quarterly meetings better still. It depends somewhat upon the number of other meetings of various kinds that require the attendance of many of the same workers. Perhaps once a quarter or once in two months is often enough as a rule; but in this case the meetings should be carefully planned, perhaps for two or three years in advance, that there may be sufficient variety in the topics, and that no important topic may be wholly neglected.

The duties of the officers of a Junior union and the work of the union itself have been so wisely stated in " The Junior Manual " by Professor Wells that I cannot do better than to quote from him.

President of the Union.—" The work of the president of the Junior union is limited only by her time and strength. She should visit as many of the societies in the union as possible, holding private talks with every superintendent, and inspiring the Juniors by brief and bright addresses. She will, of course, be the ruling spirit in the union lookout committee, guiding their work in the organization of new societies, and whenever possible be present to control the organization. She will have it among her duties to urge upon the older Endeavorers of the city the claims of Junior work, advising them to form Junior committees for the aid of the Junior superintendents.

" The planning of the rallies of the union will largely fall to her share, as well as the management of the quarterly superintendents' meetings. She must keep posted upon all recent developments of Junior methods, and must not fail to keep up an acquaintance with the Junior workers of her city or district."

" **The Secretary.**—The position of secretary of the Junior union is one of great importance. It is her task to send out notifications of the rallies and superintendents' meetings, informing the different superintendents what part, if any, they and their Juniors have in the programme, what is the theme for discussion in the superintendents' meeting, and what will be expected by way of participation from all who come. It will be her duty to correspond with whatever speakers from outside the society are obtained for the Junior rally.

" Especially it will be her task to collect the statistics of the union.   Her report should show the names and membership, active and preparatory, of all societies in the union, the date of their organization, the names and addresses of their superintendents and assistant superintendents and of the pastors of the churches with which they are connected. Additional facts which should be given are the number that have graduated from the society during the year, the number that have joined the church, the amount of money given to missions, the number of new members received during the year, and any other statistics that will be of general interest.   Large space in the report should be given to accounts of any especially helpful plans that have been tried and proved throughout the union, as well as to suggestions for fresh endeavors."

" **The Union Treasury.**—The work of a Junior union cannot be carried on without money.   The correspondence, the printing, the circular letters, the carfare of the speakers, the gifts of literature to those who are organizing new societies, all such things take money.   The entire sum necessary, however, to do a large amount of good in the course of a year's Junior work is very slight, and the Junior superintendents and societies will gladly contribute it.   Do not fail to hold to the Christian Endeavor principle of free-will contributions.   You may go so far as to announce to the societies what amount of money is required to conduct the affairs of the union in good shape, but let each society determine for itself, considering its numbers and resources, what is its own share of this sum."

" Topics for Superintendents' Meetings.—In most superintendents' meetings the problem will be what topics of burning interest to omit rather than what to talk about. However, the following list of themes for discussion may prove useful and suggestive:

The advantages of intermediate societies.

Graduation : at what age? with what ceremonies?

Your pet plan of Bible-study.

How do you arouse interest in temperance?

How do you make sure the Juniors read the daily readings?

What is your way of teaching missions ?

What committees are essential ?

How to win and hold the boys.

How to get all to sing.

Teaching Juniors to pray.

Fresh modes of carrying on the consecration meeting.

How to keep the society treasury full.

The preservation of order in the meetings.

Interesting the parents in the society.

The good of Mothers' Societies of Christian Endeavor.

How to teach the Juniors to give.

How to influence the home life of the Juniors.

What do Juniors learn about their church?

Your brightest Junior social.

How get the Juniors from preparatory to active membership.

What does the parents' pledge mean in your church?

How can we improve our union work ?

How do you present to your Juniors the claims of Christ ?

Object-lessons for Juniors.

How do you get the older Endeavorers interested in your Juniors ?

What does your society do for the Sunday-school ?

How do you receive new members ?

How do you carry on your business meetings ?

Where may new societies be organized ? "

"**The Rallies.**—At the Junior rallies the best portion of the church should be set apart for the Juniors themselves. They should wear badges, and carry at the heads of their lines their society banners. As they enter, they should sing their society marching-songs, and should sit together as societies."

Throughout the meeting let as much as possible be given to the Juniors to do. A Junior choir might furnish music, and Junior ushers should escort the company to their seats. The address of welcome should be made by a Junior from the society of the church, and the response be given by one of the visiting Juniors. Each society might in response to the roll-call rise and sing their society hymn or repeat their society motto. Throughout the longer and more formal exercises give the children something to do on every possible occasion. It will serve to hold their attention if you call upon them now and then to raise their hands in voting, to wave their handkerchiefs, to wave flags, or to rise all together.

A concert exercise by the Juniors, especially one that will require a little costuming, short papers by

Juniors, recitations, and Junior songs, either solos or choruses,—all of these will serve to make the young people feel that the meeting is their very own. Usually conclude the rally with a consecration service, the societies taking part as a whole in whatever way they see fit. At the close repeat the pledge in concert.

Many a Junior rally has been spoiled by a long harangue that does not interest or help the children. Choose your speaker only for his known ability to talk so that the children will listen and be helped. Above all, see that the programme is not too long. Save some plans for the next time.

The State Work.—In a larger way the State work is carried on in much the same manner. The State Junior superintendent should consider it her work to keep in touch with the Junior superintendents throughout the State. At the State convention she should establish a Junior headquarters, where the Junior superintendents may register and hold their conferences, as well as become acquainted with one another by social intercourse. In this room should also be arranged samples of all kinds of Junior literature and helps.

" The State superintendent's annual report should be given wide circulation. It should contain an abstract of statistics gathered, an account of the parts of the State yet needing to be roused to the importance of Junior work, an urging to missionary effort along this line, and suggestions regarding the most important methods of work. Every society in the State should receive a printed copy of this report, which should be read at some society meeting."

Questions for Review.

(*a*)   What is the object of a Junior union?
(*b*)   Who shall belong to it?
(*c*)   How often shall it meet?
(*d*)   What can it do for the superintendents?   For the
          Juniors?
(*e*)   How can it multiply societies?
(*f*)   How often shall it meet?

CHAPTER XXVII.

Number of Endeavor Societies.—According to the latest statistics (January 1, 1903) there are now in the world 45,854 Young People's Societies of Christian Endeavor and 16,387 Junior societies, a proportion of about thirty-three per cent of Junior societies. These societies are found now in almost every country in the world, and they are working in substantially the same way. To one who has had opportunity to visit societies in many lands it is wonderful to see what good work many of these foreign Juniors are doing.

One of the best Junior prayer-meetings I ever attended was in a little Chinese society in the city of Foochow, China. There were present about thirty boys and girls from six or seven to fifteen years of age, as nearly as a foreigner could judge. The meeting was led by a girl who appeared to be about thirteen or fourteen, and the reverence and earnestness shown in that meeting were such as would rejoice the heart of a Junior superintendent in America. Almost every little Chinese boy and girl in that meeting repeated a Bible verse, or answered a question, or expressed some thought on the topic ; and then they bowed their heads, and most of the older ones offered prayer ; and to the listener, who of course could not understand the words, yet could understand the spirit and the earnestness, there seemed to be a real spiritual power in that little meeting; and the missionary who spoke the closing words was so earnest, and apparently so simple in her talk, that her little listeners seemed to be not only interested but helped by her words.

Another very earnest little Junior society that I have lately seen was found in Budapest in Hungary, and their work would be an example to many of our societies in America. Many reminiscences of other little societies in Europe and Asia and Australia and in some of the islands of the seas have led to the belief that Junior Endeavor is well adapted to the children of every land, and that it is of great advantage to train up the boys and girls in this way before they enter into the work of the older society and take their places among the active workers in the church.

According to the latest statistics the Junior societies are distributed in the different lands as follows:

United States - - - -	13,872
Canada - - - - -	642
Foreign and Missionary Lands -	1,873

Proportion of Christian Endeavor and Junior Endeavor.—It will be seen from the figures given at the beginning of this chapter that the proportion of Junior societies to Christian Endeavor societies is not what it should be. If Christian Endeavor is really a good thing for young people, if it does develop and strengthen their Christian character, and train them up for service in the church, why should we wait till the boys and girls are sixteen or seventeen or eighteen before we begin their training?

A Question of Relative Importance.—In every other branch of their education there seems to be no doubt that they should begin quite young. Musicians tell us that children should begin at six or seven, or even younger, to take lessons on the piano if they would become good players. Teachers tell us that children should begin their education in the kindergarten while they are three or four years old. We have also our manual-training schools and lessons in sloyd for boys and girls in the grammar schools, and our girls must begin when they are quite small to learn to sew, and to know at least a little something about housework.

Why, then, should their religious training wait till they are seventeen or eighteen? Is it that they will take to Christian work naturally, and do not need the training and experience? Or is it that we consider their training in Christian service of less importance? Or is it, perhaps, that we have not given the matter much thought, and have never put these questions to ourselves definitely?

Trained for Service.—Why is it that there are so few willing and earnest workers in our churches? Why is it always so hard to find Sunday-school teachers and superintendents, and presidents for the various ladies' organizations, and members of committees for the various departments of church-work? Why is it that there is such a spirit of " I don't want to play, if I've got to be it " in our churches? Is it not largely because so many of our older members of the churches have not been taught and trained for Christian service, because they really do not know how to do it, or perhaps sometimes because, not having been trained to it, they have never acquired the willing spirit ?

The Junior society is an effort to remedy this state of affairs, and to train up a future generation of workers who will be willing and able to take their share of the work of the church, because they have been taught how to work, and have, while they were young, cultivated a spirit of willingness. If the Junior society can really accomplish this,—and it has already done it in some churches,—why should not there be in every church a Junior Endeavor society, which shall aim to do just this work ? Why is it that so many of our churches have a Young People's Christian Endeavor society, and no Junior society ?

How to Find a Junior Superintendent.—Perhaps the most common reason for the lack of a Junior Endeavor society in any particular church is not so much indifference, or lack of interest in the subject, as lack of a Junior superintendent. There is no doubt that the work of a Junior superintendent requires great tact and judgment, and a winning way, and ability to talk with children,—gifts which are not bestowed upon every one. It may be that the only person in any particular church who has these gifts is already overloaded, and cannot undertake anything more. Or it may be that there is really no one who seems to be fitted for the work, and those who most nearly reach the standard of perfection needed have neither the time nor strength for it. What, then, can be done?

" Find a Way or Make One."—Just look the situation fairly in the face. If this Junior work be something that ought to be done, then it should be undertaken. Take for your motto, " Either I will find a way, or make one." If there is no one else in the church who is ready to take the responsibility for starting a Junior society, then the older society should do it. If the young lady who seems to be exactly fitted for the work is too much overloaded already, ask her to consider seriously whether it would not be wiser to lay down the work that half a dozen other people ought to be doing, and to devote herself to the work of raising up twenty or thirty or more future workers who shall be ready to devote their time and strength to the work of the church when they are older.

Two or Three Superintendents.—Try for three superintendents, if need be, and perhaps their different talents will supplement one another, and together they can do a grand work for the children. It may be, for instance, that there is some young woman who is gifted in speaking to the children and helping them to lead their meetings, but cannot give the time for the committee work and other outside work. Perhaps another can take that part of the work, and another can help with the music and make herself useful in many little ways ; and so, working and planning together, they may find that three are better than one. It certainly is true that most churches as well as most individuals succeed in getting the things they want most, and any church that really wants to have a Junior society will probably succeed in having one. If a church does not really want it, then it ought to be because that church is already accomplishing the same result in a better way.

Junior Fellowship.—Our Juniors ought also to be better acquainted with one another, and their elders should in some way make this possible for them. Help them in some way to keep in touch with other societies, that they may know how other boys and girls are working for Christ, and may stimulate and help one another. Through the missionary committee it ought to be possible to exchange an occasional letter with some Junior society in mission lands, and through *The Christian Endeavor World*, or through a correspondence committee, they might learn of some Christian Endeavor methods that other boys and girls have tried that they too would be glad to try.

Some Junior societies might find it possible to provide a Christmas good time for some missionary Junior Endeavor society, and in this way get a sense of their brotherhood. Let the prayer-meeting or information committee sometimes report the work of some other Juniors, or read a letter from some foreign Junior. Keep the Juniors informed about the thousands of boys and girls all around the world who are trying to keep the same promises that they have made, and let it be true of our boys and girls that " they helped every man his neighbor."

Our Aim.—The object of all these Junior Endeavor societies is the same,—to strengthen their own Christian lives, and then to reach out and help as many other lives as possible, to make the boys and girls useful and earnest workers for Christ and the church, and to raise up a generation of consecrated, willing Christian workers in the Master's vineyard.

If this object is constantly kept in the mind of those who are working in the Junior societies, and if constant efforts through the Junior unions and other agencies are made, then we may reasonably expect that in the church of the future there will be a larger and a more earnest energetic effort made to extend the kingdom of Christ, and that some, at least, of the evils that exist in our churches to-day will be remedied. God grant that the day may come when there shall be found in every church many who shall heed the Master's words, " Suffer the little children to come unto me," and who shall earnestly try to lead the children to him, and to train them for his service.

Questions for Review.

(*a*) In what countries are Junior Endeavor societies found ?

(*b*) What ought to be the proportion between Junior and senior societies ?

(*c*) What is the most important part of a child's education ?

(*d*) Why are there so few willing workers in our churches ?

(*e*) What is the most common reason for not having a Junior society in a church ?

(*f*) How can a Junior superintendent be found ?

(*g*) How can Junior societies help one another ?

(*h*) What is our aim in all this work for the children ?

APPENDIX A.

MODEL CONSTITUTION OF THE JUNIOR SOCIETY OF CHRISTIAN ENDEAVOR.

ARTICLE I.—*Name.*

This society shall be called the JUNIOR SOCIETY OF CHRISTIAN ENDEAVOR OF..

ARTICLE II.—*Object.*

Its object shall be to promote an earnest Christian life among the boys and girls who shall become members, and prepare them for the active service of Christ.

ARTICLE III.—*Membership.*

1. The members shall consist of three classes, Active, Preparatory, and Honorary.

2. *Active Members.* Any boy or girl, who shall be approved by the Superintendent and Assistant, may become an Active Member of the society by signing the following pledge :—

ACTIVE MEMBER'S COVENANT.

Trusting in the Lord Jesus Christ for strength, I promise him that I will strive to do whatever he would like to have me do ; that I will pray and read the Bible every day ; and that, just so far as I know how, I will try to lead a Christian life. I will be present at every meeting of the society when I can, and will take some part in every meeting.

Name...

I am willing that............................. should sign this pledge, and will do all I can to help.............keep it.

Parent's name...

Residence ....

---

3. *Preparatory Members* shall be those who wish to have the help of the society, but whose parents are not yet quite ready to let them sign the active member's covenant. They will be expected to attend the meetings regularly, and it is hoped that this will be considered simply as a preparation for active membership. Any children, however young, who will be quiet during the meetings may, with the approval of the Superintendents, become Preparatory Members by signing the following pledge :—

JUNIOR CHRISTIAN ENDEAVOR PLEDGE

FOR PREPARATORY MEMBERS.

I will be present at every meeting of the society when I can, and will be quiet and reverent during the meeting.

Signed ....

4. *Honorary Members.* All mothers who are interested in the society, and who desire to help it, by their prayers, by their occasional presence, and by their hearty co-operation with the Superintendents, are invited to become Honorary Members.

The Pastor and the President of the senior society shall also be Honorary Members.

ARTICLE IV.—*Officers.*

The officers of the society shall be a Superintendent, an Assistant Superintendent, a President, a Vice-President, a Secretary, and a Treasurer. There shall be a Lookout, a Prayer-Meeting, and a Missionary Committee, and such other committees as may be needed.

ARTICLE V.—*Duties of Officers.*

1. The *Superintendent* shall have full control of the society.
2. The *Assistant Superintendent* shall aid the Superintendent in her work. The Assistant shall take care of all funds belonging to the society, the money being turned over to her by the Treasurer at the close of each meeting.
3. The *President* shall conduct the business meetings, under the direction of the Superintendent.
4. The *Vice-President* shall act in the absence of the President.
5. The *Secretary* shall keep a correct list of the members, take the minutes of the business meetings, and call the roll at each meeting.
6. The *Treasurer* shall take up the collections, enter the amount in the account-book, and turn over the money to the Assistant Superintendent, and also enter all expenditures as directed by the Superintendent.
7. The Superintendent and Assistant may be appointed by the Pastor, or by the Young People's Society (if one exists), with the approval of the Pastor. The other officers and committees shall be nominated by the Superintendent and Assistant, and elected by the society. All officers shall be chosen once a year.

ARTICLE VI.—*Duties of Committees.*

1. The *Lookout Committee* shall secure the name of any who may wish to join the society and report the same to the Superintendents for action. They shall also obtain excuses from members absent from the roll-call, and affectionately look after and reclaim any who seem indifferent to their covenant.
2. The *Prayer-Meeting Committee* shall, in connection with

the Superintendent, select topics, assign leaders, and do what it can to secure faithfulness to the prayer-meeting pledge.

3. The *Missionary Committee* shall, with the help of the Superintendents, arrange for a monthly missionary meeting, obtain subscribers to the missionary magazines, and try to interest the members in home and foreign work.

ARTICLE VII.—*Relationship.*

This society shall be closely related to the Mothers' Meeting, if there is one, and to the senior society of Christian Endeavor, and shall occasionally send a report of their work to these societies. It is expected that, when the members of the Junior society have reached their age-limit, they will enter the senior society as active members.

ARTICLE VIII.—*Meetings.*

1. A prayer-meeting shall be held once every week. A consecration meeting shall be held once a month, at which the pledge shall be read and the roll called ; and the responses of the members shall be considered a renewal of the covenant of the society. If any member is absent from three consecutive consecration meetings without excuse, his name shall be dropped from the list of members.

2. Part of the hour of the weekly meeting shall, if deemed best, be used by the Pastor or Superintendent of the society for instruction, or for other exercises which they may approve.

ARTICLE IX.—*Amendments.*

This Constitution may be amended at any regular business meeting of the society, by a two-thirds vote of the active members present.

BY-LAWS.

---

1. This society shall hold a prayer-meeting on.......................... of each week. The last regular meeting of each month shall be a consecration meeting. The business meeting may be held in connection with the first regular meeting of each month.

2. The officers and committees shall be chosen in........................ and continue a year, beginning on the first of the month following their election.

3. Special meetings of the society may be held at any time at the call of the Superintendent.

4. A collection shall be taken at the consecration meeting, and at the other meetings if desired, the money thus obtained to be held available for benevolent objects and to meet the expenses of the society.

5. All committees should meet at least once a month for consultation with the Superintendent in regard to their work.

6. All expenditures shall be made under the direction of the Superintendent.

7. Other committees may be added, whose duties shall be defined as follows :—

The *Music Committee* shall distribute and collect the singing-books, and co-operate with the leader of the meeting in trying in every way to make the singing a success.

The *Temperance Committee* shall arrange for an occasional temperance meeting, and circulate a temperance pledge among the members.

The *Sunday-school Committee* shall secure the names of children who do not attend Sunday-school and invite them to become members of the Sunday-school.

The *Flower Committee* shall provide flowers for the Sunday-school room and distribute fruit and flowers to the sick and needy.

The *Scrap-book Committee* shall collect pictures and clippings and make scrap-books for sick and disabled members and for distribution in the hospitals.

The *Relief Committee* shall collect clothing for the destitute children found in the Sunday-school and society, and bring it to the Superintendent for distribution.

The *Birthday Committee* shall report all birthdays as they occur among the members, so that special prayer may be offered for each member on his or her birthday.

The *Social Committee* shall arrange for sociables as often as it seems best, and shall invite other children to the meetings.

APPENDIX B.

HOW TO CONDUCT A BUSINESS MEETING.

By Mrs. Alice May Scudder.

Perhaps some of our Junior leaders think that the business meetings of their society are of little account, since the primal object of Christian Endeavor is to develop spirituality. Such reasoning, however, is false and harmful, for every society should aim to develop Christians who shall be physically, intellectually, commercially, as well as spiritually, of value to the world in which they live. The old-fashioned flat bouquet, beautiful only on its face, has given way to one which is round and lovely on every side, and there should also be an effort to develop the children into all-round Christians, who shall attract by their symmetric beauty.

Have a care, then, for the business meetings, as well as the prayer meetings. Let there be as perfect training in this department as in any other. "Robert's Rules of Order" is a small, inexpensive book, and has invaluable rules for parliamentary usage. From it I frequently quote.

The Juniors ought to conduct their own business meetings, and the leader should correct all errors, until the children understand the *modus operandi* as well as grown people. The following little catechism, if learned, will help them.

Whose duty is it to call a meeting to order? *Ans.* That of the president of the society.

In what words should he do so? *Ans.* He should come forward and say, "The meeting will please come to order."

What is his next duty? *Ans.* To ask whether the secretary is present; if he is not, he will ask the meeting to appoint a temporary clerk.

If the president is absent, who shall preside? *Ans.* The vice-president.

How should a motion be made? *Ans.* Before a member can make a motion or address the society, it is necessary that he *obtain the floor;* that is, he must rise and address the presiding officer by his title, "Mr. Chairman," or "Mr. President;" after which, the president will announce the member's name. Before any subject is open to debate it is necessary, first, that a motion be made; second, that it be seconded; and, third, that it be stated by the presiding officer. Then it can become a matter of debate, until such time as it seems wise to vote upon it, when some one may say to end the debate, "I call for the question," or simply, "Question."

If any one speaks improperly in a debate, what shall be done? *Ans.* Some one should say, "I call the person speaking to order."

Can a person change a motion after making it? *Ans.* If a person wishes to change a motion, he can do so, provided no one objects.

What is meant by the expression, "I move that the question be laid on the table"? *Ans.* It means that the matter under discussion shall not be talked of for the present. When it is desired to consider it again, some one may say, "I move to take it from the table."

What is a quorum? *Ans.* A quorum is such a number as is competent to transact business. Unless there is a special rule the quorum is a majority of the members.

What is the usual order followed in a business meeting? *Ans.* The usual order is:—

1. Prayer.
2. Reading the record of the previous meeting.
3. Election of officers (if it is the appointed time).
4. Reports of officers.
5. Reports of committees.
6. Unfinished business.
7. New business.
8. Prayer. Adjournment.

These we shall consider in the order named.

1. *Prayer.* This shall be short, being confined chiefly to a request for aid to carry on that specific meeting aright.

2. *Reading the Minutes of the Previous Meeting.* After these have been read the president will say, "You have heard the minutes. If there are no corrections, they will stand approved."

3. *Election of Officers.* A nominating committee is usually appointed previous to the meeting, and the president will say, "We will hear the report of our nominating committee," after which the chairman will rise and say, "Our committee would offer the names of Mr. ——, for president; Miss ——, for vice-president; Miss ——, for recording secretary; Mr. ——, for corresponding secretary; Miss ——, for treasurer."

Votes may be taken in any of the following ways, unless otherwise mentioned in the constitution : by raising the hand, by rising, by ayes and nays, or by ballot. If the latter form is adopted, the president should appoint two tellers, whose duty it is to pass the slips, to collect them after they are filled out, and, after counting them, to declare the result to the president, who shall announce it in the following manner : " The whole number of votes cast is —— ; Mr. A received —— ; Mr. B, —— ; Mr. C, —— ; Mr. B, receiving the majority, is elected." If there is only one nominee, and the feeling is unanimous, the secretary may cast one vote, which shall be for the whole membership present.

4. *Reports of Officers.* These reports should be carefully prepared, but not written in sermon style ; too many, with a desire to be very spiritual, take this time to *preach*, and it is not the proper thing to do. Don't infringe on your pastor's rights, especially in a business meeting. If reports are satisfactory, they will be accepted by vote, introduced by these words, " I move we accept the report."

5. *Reports of Regular Committees.* The monthly reports of the regular committees should be presented in writing by the chairman or by some member of the committee designated by him. No formal vote of acceptance is necessary. At the close of the meeting the reports should be handed to the secretary to be placed on file.

Reports of Special Committees. The report of a committee should be made by the chairman, who is always the first one named on the committee. It is his duty to call his committee together to talk over the matter intrusted to their care. Committee work, when brought before the president or society for approval, should be introduced thus : " The committee beg leave to submit the following report ; " and in closing say, " All of which is respectfully submitted." When the report of a committee is read, they are discharged without any motion to that effect ; but if the matter should need further attention, the same committee can be continued by a motion " to refer the matter back to the same committee."

6. *Unfinished Business.* Any business not fully completed at a previous session may come up at this point in the meeting.

7. *New Business.* All items of business to be brought forward for the first time should be presented in a clear and concise manner. Much time, and often controversy, can be avoided if the person introducing new business has the subject well in his own mind.

8. *Prayer. Adjournment.* A motion to adjourn should be made in these words : " I move we adjourn." If this is seconded, and the majority vote for it, the meeting is ended. A motion to adjourn takes precedence of all other motions.

APPENDIX C.

JUNIOR CHRISTIAN ENDEAVOR UNIONS.

By Kate H. Haus.

In union there is strength. Genuine help and inspiration come from numbers when working harmoniously under one banner for one common cause. So, wherever there are two Junior Christian Endeavor societies existing in any city, town, or village, organize a Junior union for better work, and in order to spread the good work as much and as rapidly as possible. To that end, which is the glory and honor of " Christ and the church," the following constitution and suggestions are offered:

CONSTITUTION.

ARTICLE I.—*Name*.

This organization shall be known as the Junior Christian Endeavor Union of..

ARTICLE II.—*Object*.

The object of the Union shall be to stimulate and encourage an interest in Junior Christian Endeavor work, to provide an opportunity for interchange of thought, and for improvement in methods among its leaders, to promote the growth of children in the Christian life, and to interest them in every branch of church and Sunday-school work.

ARTICLE III.—*Membership*.

Any Junior society of Christian Endeavor connected with an evangelical church or mission, working upon Christian Endeavor principles, and having the Christian Endeavor pledge, may join this Union upon its vote to do so, when such vote is approved by the pastor and the Junior superintendent, and upon the society's application for admission to the Executive Committee of the Union.

ARTICLE IV.—*Executive Committee.*

This Union shall be controlled by an Executive Committee composed of the superintendents of the Junior societies belonging to the Union, or of the chairman of the Junior committees having the Junior societies in charge. This Committee shall meet for consultation once a month, or upon the call of the President, and shall choose annually from among its members a President, a Vice-President, a Secretary, and a Treasurer, whose duties shall be those usually belonging to such officers. The pastors and assistant superintendents of the societies belonging to the Union shall constitute an Advisory Committee, which may meet for consultation with the Executive Committee, upon its request to do so.

If any society shall not have an assistant superintendent, the superintendent may appoint a member to act with the Advisory Committtee.

ARTICLE V.—*Meetings.*

There shall be a rally or mass-meeting held quarterly, or as often as the Executive Committee deem advisable. Such meetings may be devotional, social, or otherwise, at the discretion of the Executive Committee.

ARTICLE VI.—*Quorum.*

Representatives from............................. societies shall constitute a quorum for the transaction of business at any meeting of the Executive Committee.

ARTICLE VII.—*Honorary Members.*

All Christians not superintendents, but interested in the work among the children, may become honorary members of the Union by paying the sum of............................. annually or semiannually, thereby signifying their willingness to do what is in their power to advance the interests of the Union. Honorary members may be made members of the Advisory Committee.

ARTICLE VIII.—*Vote.*

Every member attending a rally or mass-meeting shall be entitled to vote upon any question that may be brought before such meeting.

ARTICLE IX.—*Finances.*

The expenditures of this Union shall be met by voluntary semi-annual contributions from the different societies belonging to it, and by collections taken for this purpose at any of the mass-meetings or rallies.

ARTICLE X.—*Relation to Christian Endeavor Union.*

Since the Junior Christian Endeavor work is closely allied to the work of the Young People's Society of Christian Endeavor, it is expected that the President of the Christian Endeavor Union shall have a voice in all the deliberations of the Junior Union, and the President of the Junior Union shall have the like privilege in all the deliberations of the Christian Endeavor Union, in order that the two Unions may work in harmony and to the best interests of the Christian Endeavor cause in the city.

ARTICLE XI.—*Amendments.*

This constitution may be altered or amended by a vote of ....of the Executive Committee, when deemed advisable, at any session of the Executive and Advisory Committees jointly convened for that purpose.

SUGGESTIVE PROGRAMMES FOR RALLIES.

1. Praise service, led by a Junior member.
2. Three-minute papers upon Junior work, by Juniors of different societies.
    a. Work of the prayer-meeting committee.
    b. Looking after delinquent members.
    c. Missionary work.
3. Open parliaments of five minutes each upon the papers.
4. Song.
5. Recitation, concert or individual.
6. Instrumental music, by a Junior or Juniors.
7. Open parliament : "Good Citizenship and Temperance."
8. Song.
9. Chalk-talk.
10. Roll-call of societies.
11. Song, during which the collection may be taken.
12. Short consecration service.
13. Closing prayer and song.   Mizpah benediction.

The whole programme may occupy from an hour to an hour and a half, or longer if wished.

Another programme may be composed of musical and literary selections and concert recitations representing the different societies belonging to the Union.

Another programme may be an Easter or Christmas service.

Another may be a temperance or missionary service.

Another may be an anniversary or pledge service, as published by the United Society of Christian Endeavor.

Another may be a service that shall teach loyalty to one's country, her flag, and all recognized institutions that promote her welfare.

At all these rallies have the societies bring their banners and flags, and wear their badges.   Make the preparations for them as carefully and completely as you would for the largest convention.

APPENDIX D.

CATECHISMS IN JUNIOR SOCIETIES.

FOR THE CONSIDERATION OF PASTORS AND JUNIOR SUPERINTENDENTS.

BY REV. FRANCIS E. CLARK.

There ought to be in every Junior Endeavor society some form of catechetical instruction. A good plan would be to use for ten minutes of each Junior meeting manuals of question and answer, in which the boys and girls may learn the doctrines of their own church, its history, and its work, and also lessons in clean, upright living, obedience, reverence, humility, and faithfulness.

I do not know how this can be done in any other way so well as by some manual of instruction, which used to be called " the catechism," and for which there is still no better name.

WHAT IS ADVOCATED.

I hope it will be fully understood, however, that I do not advocate giving all the time, or even most of it, to this instruction. The Junior society is chiefly for *training*.

Children can be taught to pray only by praying, and to work by working, and to express their love for Christ by expressing it in some simple, natural, childlike way ; and it is still necessary and always will be necessary to devote much of the Junior hour to the prayer-meeting and much of the strength of the Junior society to the committees, the lookout, and the social, and the flower, and the sunshine committees, and all the others which furnish the indispensable and absolutely necessary means of child-training.

But at the same time I think that at least ten minutes of every hour might with profit be used for instruction by question and answer, where the answers should be carefully learned, concerning the great doctrines of the church, its history and purpose, and the practical concerns of daily life which result from these teachings.

But do you ask, Where is the perfect catechism that I shall use ?

Your denominational publishing-house undoubtedly will furnish you with at least one good one, and perhaps with a round dozen ; and in this, as in everything else, Christian Endeavor will remember its principles, that each society is to be true to its own denomination, its teaching, history, and polity. In matters of life and practice, to be sure, all denominations agree, and manuals of Scripture teaching with the answers in Bible words are already published by the United Society, and can be had for a few cents.

FITTING FOR CHURCH-MEMBERSHIP.

Some pastors and superintendents may deem it best to concentrate this catechetical instruction into six or eight weeks of the year instead of using ten minutes each week ; that is, they will give the whole hour to the catechism for a few weeks, and the rest of the year to the training idea. In either case this catechism of doctrines and duties will furnish a splendid preparation for church-membership, and every year an intelligent class of earnest, intelligent Junior Christians may be fitted for the church.

What a wide and important field does this open ! How easily in this way may our children be taught not only what their church believes, but what it stands for in history, something about the great men who have made its history, and something as well about the church universal and the martyrs and heroes who belong to all branches of it ! How plainly it can be made to appear that right living and pure thinking and honesty and reverence and faithfulness and obedience are all connected vitally with the religion of Christ !

LEARN IT.

I think the answers to the questions should be *learned* week by week. This will bring about a revival of the too much neglected art of memorizing Scripture passages and important truths framed in other words as well. The Juniors usually stay in the same society three or four or five years; and during these years, if only one question is taken up and answered and thoroughly learned and explained each hour, a very large amount of gospel truth can be inculcated.

A list of many of the leading catechisms that have been prepared may be secured from the United Society of Christian Endeavor. I am not advocating any particular catechism, or any particular way of teaching it ; but I am concerned for the introduction of the idea, and still more earnestly for the right proportion and adjustment of the two great ideas for which the Junior Endeavor society has always stood, instruction and training, teaching and practice. Stand for these two elements in your Junior society, and you will build up symmetrical, well-rounded, beautiful Christian characters, and a multitude of your boys and girls will come into the church of Jesus Christ intelligently prepared to do their duty as valiant twentieth-century Christians.

APPENDIX E.

THINGS TO REMEMBER ABOUT A JUNIOR MEETING.

By Mrs. Alice May Scudder.

Some Things Not To Do.

Do not go to a children's meeting worrying about its success.
No amount of worriment ever added to its attractiveness.
Give plenty of time for preparation, and go with a bright, cheerful heart.

Don't scold. God and the children will leave if you do.
Have plenty of helpers to keep order; but, if by chance the
number is insufficient, excuse the troublesome children quietly
before the meeting commences, by saying to them that, since
they need a sort of private watchman and none is at hand, they
may be excused until next week. Allow them to remain on a
promise of good behavior.

Do not go unprepared. It is cruel. It is not fair to ask children to leave their bats, balls, skates, and pleasant games to
come in and sit while a leader scratches for ideas. It would be
about the same thing as to ask people to dinner, and then to go
ransacking every closet to find only odds and ends to set before
them. Have good food, plenty of it, and rightly prepared, and
the children will eat. I mean, of course, spiritual food.

Don't talk or pray too long. The army beatitude, "Blessed
are they that speak short," applies admirably to Christian Endeavor work. You can't present all the needs of the universe in
a prayer service for children, nor must you exhaust too much
time in giving advice—even good advice.

Things to Do.

Be alive. "With all thy heart, with all thy soul, and with
all thy mind." This must be the spirit of every leader of children. There is no danger whatever of having too much
life, but I have more than once seen dull people who have

spoiled a meeting. I feel all the time like saying, "Wake up! Wake up!"

Be rested. Don't exhaust your nervous force any more than is absolutely necessary on the day of the meeting, for you will need a large reserve in readiness to draw upon.

Be childlike. The simpler the language, and the more suited for children the illustrations are, the better the meeting. This is much better understood now than formerly ; in fact, everything seems to aid now in making it easy for children to be religious.

Be hopeful. The work of Christianizing children is not done in a day, nor even a week, nor sometimes for years. The sculptor chisels a bit at a time, and by and by a figure of matchless beauty stands out before him. If you feel discouraged, glance back a year, and see the spiritual earnestness of these boys who once were so restless and so hard to interest. That dear timid little girl, who fairly trembled from head to foot when reading a verse, leads the meeting now with little trouble to herself or you. There are sometimes days of discouragement, but no work ever brought forth better results. Scripture says truly, "First the blade, then the ear, after that the full corn in the ear."

Excuse Card.

To be taken by the lookout committee to any members who are absent from the meeting, asking them to write the reason of their absence.

....was absent from the

last meeting because ....

....

....

Signed ....

Questions on the Pledge.

To be answered in writing by those who wish to become active members.

1. If you sign this pledge, what six things do you promise?

2. Does signing this pledge mean that you will begin now to be a Christian?

3. When you say, "I will be present at every meeting 'if I can,'" what do you mean by "if I can"?

4. What excuse could you rightly give for staying away from the meeting?

5. What does it mean to "take some part in the meeting"?

THE ROLL OF HONOR.

In some societies it is the custom to have a "roll of honor" as a help in keeping order in the meetings. A wooden board is prepared, into which little brass hooks have been screwed, as many hooks as there are children in attendance at the meetings. When a child has been present at four meetings, and has been quiet and reverent, and so far as known has been honorable in his behavior outside of the meetings, a card with his name on it is hung on this board. The effort is made to have all the children keep their names on this honor roll, and their attention is often called to it. Any one who stays away from a meeting without a sufficient reason, or is troublesome in the meeting, or is known to dishonor his society outside the meeting, must have his name taken off the roll, and it requires four weeks of good behavior to get it back again. In some societies this plan has been found to be a real help in securing faithful attendance and good behavior in the meetings.

APPENDIX F.

HOW TO ORGANIZE A MOTHERS' SOCIETY OF CHRISTIAN ENDEAVOR.

By Mrs. A. B. Fellows.

We are not astonished at the interest manifested in the Mothers' Society of Christian Endeavor and the demand that comes to us from all over the country to know how to organize such a society, for we feel that the leaven is working and the way will be opened. We are indeed grateful to know of the awakened interest in the hearts of many mothers concerning a higher spiritual standard in their homes and a desire to combine their efforts in order to bring this about.

The question now arises, "How can we organize a Mothers' society of Christian Endeavor?" You must first get the mothers with one accord in one place, by issuing a call from the pulpit, or by personal invitation, or both. Then have some one present the necessity of such an organization and try to awaken them to their responsibilities as mothers in their homes, and also as helpers in the Junior work. The pastor, or Junior superintendent (if a Junior Christian Endeavor society exists in your church), or both, will readily realize the importance and possibilities of such an organization, and should present it to the mothers. Then organize with a president, a vice-president, a secretary, and committees—also a *pledge* and constitution. Each society has, of course, the privilege of adopting their own pledge and constitution, but you may look favorably upon one that has been adopted by many societies. Meet monthly on some week-day, as best suits your convenience. The meeting should be devotional and full of praise and prayer the first half-hour. Let every member take part in some way, with sentence prayers, with a passage of Scripture, or perhaps with a bit of poetry or quotation bearing upon the topic. The last half-hour could be devoted to education on all subjects that influence the home.

May the work go forward until this society shall compass the globe. "When mothers realize the scope of motherhood, there is hope for the world."

APPENDIX G.

CONSTITUTION OF THE MOTHERS' SOCIETY OF CHRISTIAN ENDEAVOR.

ARTICLE I.—*Name*.

This society shall be called the Mothers' Society of Christian Endeavor of the........................Church of [city]........................

ARTICLE II.—*Purposes*.

The object of this society shall be to stimulate mothers to raise the standard of the Christian home, and to pray for aid to help in their Christian life the children, especially those who belong to the Junior Society of Christian Endeavor.

ARTICLE III.—*Membership*.

SECTION I. Any woman interested in the welfare of children may become a member of this society by signing the following pledge :—

Trusting in the Lord Jesus Christ for strength, I promise him that I will strive to do whatever he would have me do ; especially that I will endeavor to bring the children to Christ and to train them for him. To this end I will co-operate with the Junior Christian Endeavor superintendents in any way I can. I promise to seek daily the Master's blessing on the children. I will attend each meeting of the Mothers' Society of Christian Endeavor, unless prevented by a reason that I can conscientiously give to my Saviour, and will come prepared to add to the interest of the meeting. When obliged to be absent from the consecration meeting, I will send, if possible, a message to be read in response to my name.

Name..

Address..

Date..

SECTION 2. The relation of the Mothers' Society to the Junior Society of Christian Endeavor should be close and intimate, and it is expected that the members will in every way possible seek to promote the spiritual growth of the boys and girls of their church and Sunday-school as well as of the Junior society.

ARTICLE IV.—*Officers.*

SECTION 1. The officers of the society shall be a President, a Vice-President, and a Secretary, and such other officers as may be necessary.

SECTION 2. The President shall keep especial watch over the interests of the society, and it shall be her care to see that the committees perform the duties devolving upon them.

SECTION 3. The Vice-President shall assist the President in her duties and perform them in her absence.

SECTION 4. The Secretary shall keep a record of the names and addresses of the members, and the minutes of all prayer and business meetings, and perform the other usual duties of a Secretary.

SECTION 5. The officers and committees shall be elected by the society, and shall be chosen once a year, at the first meeting in [month] ....

ARTICLE V.—*Committees.*

SECTION 1. The Lookout Committee shall bring new members into the society, and shall do its utmost to see that the pledge is faithfully observed.

SECTION 2. The Prayer-Meeting Committee shall select topics and assign leaders for the meetings.

SECTION 3. Other committees may be added and duties undertaken according to the needs of the society.

SECTION 4. Each chairman shall bring a written report of what her committee has done during the past month, and read it at each meeting. The chairman of all standing committees, with the officers of the society, shall comprise the executive committee. All important matters of business shall be first considered by this committee and by it reported to the society for action.

ARTICLE VI.—*Meetings.*

SECTION 1. The prayer-meetings shall be held...................... of each month. At least once in three months a consecration meeting shall be held, at which the pledge shall be read and the names of members called, and the response shall be considered a renewal of the pledge.

Section 2.   Special prayer-meetings or business meetings of the society may be held at any time, at the call of the president.

Section 3.   The committees should meet at least once a month with the president, for consultation with regard to their work.

Article VII.— *Withdrawals.*

Members of the Mothers' Society who find it impossible to perform the duties of the society, or who for any reason wish to withdraw, can do so at any time by signifying their desire to the secretary ; and their names shall be taken from the list of members.

Article VIII.—*Amendments.*

This constitution may be amended at any business meeting of the society, by a two-thirds vote of all the members present, provided notice of the proposed amendment shall have been given at some previous business or prayer-meeting.

APPENDIX H.

MOTHERS' SOCIETY OF CHRISTIAN ENDEAVOR.

EDUCATIONAL TOPICS FOR PRAYER-MEETINGS.

1. LESSONS FROM THREE MOTHERS,—Hannah, Mary, and the mother of Samson. Prov. 31 : 28.

Every mother is a sacred instrument in the hand of the Creator. Get an understanding of the measureless forces from which you can draw.

2. THE POWER OF EXAMPLE IN OUR HOMES. Heb. 12 : 1.

Our lives are an open book, read attentively by the occupants of our homes. Is our conversation in heaven? Can our standard of living be questioned? How can we raise the standard?

3. OUR CHILDREN'S OBEDIENCE. I Sam. 3 : 3–10.

What kind of a parent is worthy of obedience? How to win obedience. The sad results if we fail in this.

4. GOOD CHEER AT HOME. John 15 : 11.

What makes a happy home? How is household joy frequently marred? How take the first step towards changing a sad to a joyous home?

5. TEACHING THE CHILDREN. Ps. 32 : 8.

What things should a child learn at home? How may a mother get time to teach her children? What are the rewards of such efforts?

6. MINISTRY OF SUFFERING IN OUR HOMES. Matt. 26 : 39.

There are no heights without depths. Paths that tend upward are paths of sacrifice. First the cross ; then the crown.

7. Self-Control in the Home. Heb. 12 : 1–3.

Gain it by consecration and meditation, continually looking towards our Ideal, who will carry us beyond the storms of passion into a haven of peace. Consider such an example in the home, and the atmosphere it would create.

8. The Bible in the Home. Ps. 119 : 54.

How may we exalt the Bible in our homes? What means can we take to inspire love for it in our children?

9. A Growing Home. Ps. 84 : 7.

The effect on the children when father and mother stop growing mentally and spiritually. How we can widen the home life.

10. Reading. Prov. 4 : 7.

Read for culture, information, and discipline. Bring the companionship of large souls into the home through the Bible, history, and science ; and you will thus cultivate a love for the beautiful, the true, the good.

11. Christian Courtesy. 1 Pet. 3 : 8.

How can we best teach children to be courteous and compassionate? By the Word, by our example, and by developing in them all the Christian graces. All refinement, all culture, all purity of heart, are embodied in *Christian* courtesy.

12. Faults, and How to Correct Them. Jas. 1 : 4, 5.

Our children's common faults. Injurious ways of fault-finding. The kind of fault-finding that truly corrects.

Index

JUNIOR CHRISTIAN ENDEAVOR SUPPLIES

Junior Carols. 156 hymns, besides special exercises, responsive readings, etc. Words-and-music edition, nicely bound in cloth, by express at purchaser's expense 25 cents a copy; sample copy, postpaid, 30 cents. Words-only edition, in quantities, 10 cents; sample copy, postpaid, 11 cents.

Our hymn-book for Juniors was published at great expense, and is an idea book for its purpose, The old favorites — the ones that children love to sing — are all found, and nearly 100 entirely new pieces that will win instant favor. The sections for Christmas, Easter, and other special occasions are unusually strong. The book contains 157 hymns, besides special exercises and responsive readings. Bound in blue cloth.

Junior Efficiency Wall Charts.

The Junior Chart is now printed in two colors (red and black), and is very attractive. It should be in every society where the Efficiency Campaign has been introduced. It will add encouragement to the work. Size, 14 x 22 inches. The convenient size of this chart makes it ideal for Junior workers to use. There are no sticks to break, and it can easily be rolled. It contains the Junior standards together with thermometer in the center for marking. This chart adds enthusiasm to the work of Junior efficiency, and should have a place in every Junior prayer-meeting room. The boys and girls delight in these charts because of their usefulness in the campaign of efficiency. Sold complete, with stars and tape for marking, at 50 cents each, postpaid.

Junior Text-Book.

The Junior Text-Book contains twenty-three chapters in question-and-answer form, on all the Junior officers and committees. It is the latest and most complete book out on the work for Juniors.

Many Junior superintendents will hail this book with delight because it appears at an opportune time, and it is up to date.

The book is beautifully bound in attractive green cloth, and is stamped in harmony of color that will please. The size of the book is 5 x 7½ inches, and there are one hundred pages. Price, 50 cents, postpaid.

JUNIOR BADGE

	EACH		EACH
Gold	$1.00	Gold and Enamel	$1.00
Silver	.25	Silver and Enamel	.30
Corinthian Silver	.15	Corinthian Silver and Enamel	.20

JUNIOR PLEDGE FOR CHAPEL WALL

Trusting in the Lord Jesus Christ for strength, I promise Him that I will strive to do whatever He would like to have me do: that I will pray and read the Bible every day, and that, just so far as I know how, I will try to lead a Christian life. I will be present at every meeting of the society when I can, and will take some part in every meeting.

INSPIRE THE CHILDREN

There is nothing that will inspire the boys and girls in the Junior society more than a *Junior Wall-Pledge* in the prayer-meeting room. It represents the goal that they have promised to strive to attain. The illustrations on this page will be helpful in ordering the right kind of *Junior Pledge-Card* to correspond with the wall-pledge. The reading is the same. These pledges are attractive. Occasionally we hear of Junior societies who do not use these pledges, and it is to be regretted because they are essential to the best working society, and ensure a frequent application and confession of the things the Juniors have promised to do. No Junior society should dispense with these Junior pledges. Note prices quoted on illustration.

Price, postpaid, 75 cents

JUNIOR BOOKS

Bible Chains. By Amos R. Wells. 76 pp. Cloth, 35 cents, postpaid.

This selection of Bible verses was first put out in a pamphlet for the Juniors; but it was thought to be equally helpful for adults, and for their convenience it now appears as a very attractive cloth-bound book of 76 pages. It contains 300 of the most helpful verses in the Bible, arranged for committing to memory. They are grouped under 33 leading topics, such as temptation, sorrow, purity, contentment, patience, peace, labor — just the topics on which we need to store our memories with the great Bible words, that they may lift us over the hard places of life. This is a book that all Christians will enjoy owning and using. Spare minutes could not be better employed than in adding to one's mind-treasury these 300 golden verses.

Bible in Lesson and Story, The. By Ruth Mowry Brown. 254 pp. Handsomely illustrated with twelve full-page engravings. Bound in royal purple cloth, with illuminated title in gold. Postpaid, $1.25.

To write forty chapters upon as many Bible truths, and to write each chapter in a manner that will especially interest the children, are features of this book. It contains a delightful illustrative story, together with a "Memory Gem" and an "Occupation," in which the children are given something to do that will help impress the truths that have been taught.

The suggestions for object-lessons to impress the stories and lessons upon the mind are wise in that many of them give the children something to do. — *The Outlook.*

Child's Quiet Hour, A. By Emily Williston. Cloth. Handsome cover design. Price, 35 cents, postpaid.

A delightful and helpful book of meditation, Bible reading and prayer, and new to the companions of the Quiet Hour. A well-wrought-out book of suggestions for mother and child during the Quiet Hour period. Contains Bible verses and prayers for each day in the month, with blank space for child's name. Also spaces for names of relatives, friends, teachers, pastor, missionaries, and others for whom the child will pray.

Collection Habit, The. By Amos R. Wells. Cloth, 25 cents, postpaid.

"The Collection Habit," by Amos R. Wells, is a book for workers in Junior and Intermediate societies, urging them to utilize in their work with the boys and girls the universal tendency of young people to form collections. The book shows just how the superintendent may stimulate the collecting habit, guiding it in wise directions and making it helpful to the work of the society. Many kinds of collections are described, with references to books that give further information. As a sample, the collecting of minerals is treated fully by the author, who describes all the common minerals, showing how they may be recognized and giving many practical lessons that may be drawn from them by the superintendent in the prayer meetings.

Enjoyable Entertainments. By Lilian M. Heath. 184 pp. Profusely illustrated and beautifully printed and bound. It is a handsome volume. Price, $1.00, postpaid.

This new book is a splendid achievement. It is a book for the platform, not a book of games. It will be useful for societies and Sunday-schools that wish to make money by giving a public entertainment. There is a great variety in these entertainments. There are "A Millinery Marvel," "Mother Goose Market," "High Jinks Along the Milky Way," "The Beggar Prince," "A Window Evening," "Dandelion Drill," "A Cradle-Song Concert," "A Seven Days' Wonder," "The Snow Brigade," and many other pleasurable affairs, thirty-three in all.

Good Times with the Juniors. By LILIAN M. HEATH. 178 pp. Cloth, 50 cents, postpaid.

To have good times with the little men and women of to-day is one of the greatest joys to those privileged to participate. This book adds many new things that Juniors will enjoy. It is filled with suggestions for socials, entertainments, receptions, drills, etc., besides giving several character sketches or plays for little folks. The different holidays, such as Christmas, Thanksgiving, Independence Day, Washington's Birthday, Valentine Day, etc., are all remembered. Each programme is complete in itself. Every Junior superintendent should have one of these books.

Junior Manual, The. By AMOS R. WELLS. 304 pp. Cloth, $1.25; board covers, 75 cents, postpaid.

In 304 closely printed pages and 40 chapters Mr. WELLS takes up and treats thoroughly all phases of work in religious societies for children. While particularly adapted to Junior and Intermediate societies of Christian Endeavor, it will prove helpful to Epworth Leagues and Baptist Unions. The volume is not theoretical in any part, but gathers up the plans that have actually been found useful in thousands of societies. The superintendent's work is considered in all its branches, and in short every possible form of this necessary and difficult work.

Junior Recitations. By AMOS R. WELLS. 128 pp. Cloth, 50 cents, postpaid.

This book is different from other volumes of recitations for children in having full directions for speaking prefixed to each piece. These directions relate to all kinds of unique interpretations of the recitations, by objects, placards, gestures, and other ways, and they add much to the effectiveness of the presentation. The selections cover the various holidays, such as New Year, Christmas, Thanksgiving, Fourth of July, the harvest season, Children's Day, Valentine's Day, Easter, etc. It also contains recitations, dialogues, and exercises written especially for it by Mr. WELLS.

Manual of Physical Training, A. By WILLIAM G. ANDERSON, M.D., Dr. P. H., and WILLIAM L. ANDERSON. Handsomely bound, profusely illustrated. 145 pp. Price, $1.00, postpaid.

A book just suited to the needs of those who wish to introduce the novelty of physical training in their society work; to public-school teachers, to parents, and to all young folks interested in athletics. The book does not presuppose a gymnasium or any apparatus except now and then the very simplest, such as is easily bought or made. In addition there are wise chapters on the moral and physical side of physical training, on hygiene, on home training, on habits, on first aid to the injured, on the development of the chest. A timely book.

Object-Lessons and Illustrated Talks. By Rev. GEORGE F. KENN-GOTT. 76 pp. Heavy paper covers, 25 cents, postpaid.

A very interesting presentation of a series of object lessons and illustrated talks. Superintendents of Junior and Intermediate societies will appreciate this book. Fifty-three different topics are discussed in an admirable way.

Using the Book with the Juniors. Compiled by KARL LEHMANN.

A book of the best Bible drills for use in work with boys and girls and older young people. This little book is full of valuable suggestions as to methods whereby the Bible may be made more real and helpful to young people. Price, 15 cents each.

UNITED SOCIETY OF CHRISTIAN ENDEAVOR

31 Mt. Vernon St., Boston, Mass.   405 Association Bldg., Chicago, Ill.

.